PALESTINE
STILL A DILEMMA

FRANK C. SAKRAN

AMERICAN COUNCIL ON THE MIDDLE EAST
P.O. Box 19227
Washington, D.C. 20036

Library of Congress Catalog Card Number: 76-29879

SECOND PRINTING 1978

ii

To Ann

My wife, helper, and adviser, who contributed much of her time and talent to the writing of this book.

Contents

	Preface	vii
I	The Roots of the Problem: Christianity vs. Judaism	1
II	The Expanding War: "From a Little Acorn"	12
III	The Third Jewish Invasion of Palestine	17
IV	Exit Britain; Enter the United States	28
V	Palestine at the United Nations	30
VI	Born in Blood	35
VII	Soviet Penetration Begins	44
VIII	The Aswan Dam and the Suez War	46
IX	A Decade of Peace and Decline	50
X	To War, To War	57
XI	The Drums of War Beat Louder	65
XII	The Expansionist Plans Unveiled	73
XIII	Peace: How To Prevent It	76
XIV	The Internal Arab Situation	84
XV	The October War	89
XVI	The Palestinians' Claim To Palestine	104
XVII	The Zionists' Claim	108

XVIII The "Promised Land" Argument 109

XIX The Fulfillment 121

XX The Glory and the Decline
of the Israelites 131

XXI Recapitulations 135

XXII Conclusions 138

XXIII The "Homeless Jew" and His
"Historic Connection" with Palestine 146

XXIV The Balfour Declaration and the Mandate 150

XXV The United Nations Partition Resolution 152

XXVI The Rebel Child 154

XXVII The Triumph of the P.L.O.
and Yasser Arafat 162

XXVIII Peace: Is It Possible? 169

Preface

The Truth Shall Make You Free

The half-a-century-old Palestine conflict, originally between the Palestinians and the Zionist immigrants, has twice
caused the United States to alert its mighty forces on land, on
sea, and in the air for war with the Soviet Union. And it still
threatens to ignite the dreaded nuclear conflagration. The
highly dramatized and widely publicized Kissinger "shuttle
diplomacy" did succeed in separating the warring forces after
the U.N. had imposed a cease-fire in 1973, but it has accomplished nothing else. Nearly three years have elapsed since
Kissinger arrogated unto himself—and to himself alone—the
task of mediating a peaceful settlement; but nothing has yet
been settled.

The danger of war is still present, and by committing the
United States to supply more sophisticated weapons to Israel,
Kissinger has made certain that the next war will be more
devastating. Israel has already achieved nuclear capability
and has asked Washington for Pershing missiles to deliver the
bombs. Egypt has vowed to follow suit.

News dispatches from various capitals and the voting at the
U.N. since the 1967 Arab-Israeli war show that the nations of
the world have become polarized into two camps: Israel and
the United States, plus Bolivia and the Dominican Republic

and, lately, South Africa are in one; the Arabs and the rest of the world, including the three most populous nations—China, India, and the Soviet Union—are in the other.

Despite Washington's deep involvement in this war, the billions of taxpayers' dollars Washington has poured into it, and the great danger it poses to world peace, few Americans really know the basic issues involved or understand why the United States now finds itself in a corner practically alone with Israel. The task of getting the facts has not been easy. The communications media have not always been evenhanded. Although there has been some improvement lately, the Palestinians are still called "terrorists"—without examining the reasons why they resort to terrorist tactics—and the great holy shrine of Islam—Al Haram-al-Sherif—which contains the Mosque of Omar and the Dome of the Rock, is lately being called the "Temple Mount" by the press. The book-publishing industry also, perhaps unintentionally, has been guilty of a sort of cover-up.

In *Palestine Dilemma,* published in 1948 (banned by the Zionists), this writer gave a concise history of Palestine up to 1947 when the British, frustrated, gave up the League of Nations mandate over Palestine and asked the United Nations to untangle the sorry web that they had woven. The present volume recites the tragic—and predictable—events that have transpired since that time and their widening repercussions. It examines the basic issues of the conflict and the claims of Arabs and Jews to Palestine.

The author has also dared offer a peace plan, knowing full well that both he and his plan will be roundly condemned by both sides: the Arabs will say that Palestine is theirs and that the suggested plan gives them only a part of it; the Israelis, hungry for more territory, will, of course, oppose any plan that does not satisfy their grandiose dreams. To both I say that this plan offers the best alternative to continued war, which is likely to destroy both of you and—I shudder to say it—the world as we know it. So please, don't bring down the roof on all of us as Samson did three thousand years ago.

—F.C.S.

Were all the power, that fills
the world with terror,
Were half the wealth, bestowed
on camps and courts,
Given to redeem the
human mind from error,
There were no need of arsenals
and forts:

The warrior's name would be a name
abhorréd!
And every nation, that should lift again
Its hand against a brother, on its
forehead
Would wear for evermore the
curse of Cain!

—Henry Wadsworth Longfellow
in "The Arsenal at Springfield"

I

The Roots of the Problem: Christianity vs. Judaism

Most people ascribe the Arab-Israeli conflict to the creation of the state of Israel in 1948. Some go back a little farther and blame the 1917 Balfour Declaration, while others say the culprit was Dr. Theodor Herzl and the Zionist Organization which he created two decades earlier.

These events do show the beginning and development of the confrontation between Arab and Jew in Palestine, which has resulted in four destructive wars between the two peoples who had previously lived side by side in peace.

Actually, however, the present struggle between the Arabs and the Jews is rooted in the two-thousand-year-old conflict between the Jews and the Christian world. For, were it not for this conflict, Zionism would never have been born and the Jews would not have had a desire to emigrate to Palestine, the small country with very limited resources that most of their ancestors left voluntarily to seek greener pastures.

Some writers assert that the present struggle between Arab and Jew is a continuation of the war between the Hebrews and the Canaanites for control of the country. It is true that a large segment of the Palestinians fighting Israel today are the descendants of the Canaanites and Philistines who resisted the invasion of their homeland by the Hebrews some three

1

thousand years ago. But that war was ended by the removal of ten of the twelve Hebrew tribes to Assyria, where they were totally and irrevocably assimilated, and the subsequent expulsion of the remaining two tribes, Judah and Benjamin, by the Romans. Two thousand years elapsed between this event and the beginning of the Arab-Jew conflict.

Would a people scattered over the globe and speaking a hundred different tongues, united only by the slender tie of the designation *Jew*, start a war against a hitherto friendly nation for the purpose of taking part of that nation's territory simply because some of their ancestors lived there in ancient times? Let us not forget that most of the Jews in Israel today are not racially pure. And many of them are avowed atheists and have no sentimental or spiritual attachment to the land. Moreover, these Jews did not choose to settle in Judea, the ancient home of their ancestors, but in "Galilee of the gentiles" and in the home of the ancient Philistines on the coast.

We think not. The Jews are a practical people. They had to have more than a vague and uncertain sentimental reason to respond to the call of the Zionist leaders. Obviously this reason was their inability to find peace and tranquility in Christian Europe. This is shown by the fact that most of the early Jewish immigrants to Palestine came from those countries where anti-Jewish feeling was strong and that the Zionist movement did not show great success prior to the rise of the Nazi Regime in Germany.

This raises the question why the Jews have not found peace and happiness in Christendom.

This is a difficult question to answer. Most Jews will say the conflict is religious and the product of religious bigotry. Some say it is anti-Semitism, implying that all antagonism toward them is due to racial bigotry. Of course the early conflict was religious. Jesus and his disciples often attacked the Jewish hierarchy's teachings. The priests of Yahweh and the Pharisees, etc., rose up against him and his early followers. We are told that St. Paul, before his conversion to Christian-

2

ity, busied himself scouring the country and flushing out Christians. When Christianity became the state religion of the Roman Empire, the Jews began to pay heavily for rejecting Jesus. This religious antagonism continued for centuries.

But surely Hitler's hatred of Jews was not born of excessive Christian zeal.

Likewise, the Russian anti-Semitism of which the Jews complain today cannot be said to be a part of the ancient conflict between Christianity and Judaism. Communism, as we all know, mocks all religions. And many of the founders of Communism in that country were Jews. Indeed, the founder of Communism, Karl Marx, was a Jew. Nor can it be attributed to racial bigotry. Russia is a nation of many races, cultures, and traditions.

Whatever the cause, the fact is that the Jews have had trouble living with other races or other religious persuasions from the beginning of their recorded history. A brief review of this history is in order here.

According to the Bible, when the children of Israel came out of Egypt under the leadership of Moses, they were one nation and were considered such by the Egyptians and by the people through whose territory they passed. Although they consisted of twelve separate tribes, they claimed descent from a common ancestor, Jacob or Israel. They traveled together and roamed the wilderness for forty years as one people called "Israel," a reference to their ancestor.

They invaded the land of Canaan as one nation under a single commander, Joshua. But soon after being established there, the Bible begins to speak of them as "Judah and Israel."

When their first king, Saul, a Benjamite, ordered a census to ascertain his actual fighting strength before going into battle, he was told that "Israel" had three hundred thousand men and "Judah" thirty thousand (I Sam. 11:8).

This separateness was soon to develop into a complete break and open warfare.

Upon the death of Saul during a battle with the Philistines,

3

a member of the tribe of Judah named David, supported by his own tribe, wrested the crown of Israel from the house of Saul after several engagements and was recognized as king of all the tribes.

The Old Testament sheds no light on the cause of the separation of Judah from the other tribes of Israel. However, its silence lends strong support to the historians who say that the Hebrews, or Israelites, were not originally one nation and did not enter Palestine together at one time as the book of Joshua says. It seems they were different tribes, perhaps unrelated, but spoke a common language. They migrated to Palestine at different periods and later formed a league against the indigenous peoples, especially the Philistines, who not only stopped their advance but defeated them, disarmed them, and exacted tribute from them.

It seems that one of these tribes, Judah, never did agree to a complete merger with the others. But while it was willing to join them in war against the common enemy, it nevertheless kept its separate identity.

This alliance between Judah and Israel was short-lived. A feeling of resentment simmered among the men of Israel who were much larger in numbers than Judah but now found themselves ruled by a Jewish king.

The situation was aggravated by David's son and successor, Solomon, who levied heavy taxes upon the people for his building program and the maintainance of his court in dazzling splendor. He had "seven hundred wives of royal ranks and three hundred concubines" in the royal palace.

We are told that upon the death of Solomon, his son Rehoboam ascended the throne at Jerusalem. He then went to the ancient city of Schechem, which already was regarded as the political center of ten of the tribes, to be crowned king over these northern tribes, Israel, whose leaders had pointedly ignored the coronation ceremonies held at Jerusalem. Before taking the oath of allegiance to him, the assembled leaders of these tribes asked him, "Thy father made our yoke grievous:

4

now therefore ease thou somewhat the grievous servitude of thy father, and his heavy yoke that he put upon us, and we will serve thee" (II Chron. 10:4 KJV).

Just what is this heavy yoke of which they complained is not clear. But it does not appear to have been slave labor. Solomon did order "three score and ten thousand [men] ... to be bearers of burden, and four score thousand to be in the mountains" (to cut stones) (II Chron. 2:18 KJV). However, these appear to have been drafted from among the conquered peoples. Second Chronicles 8:9 KJV says, "But of the children of Israel did Solomon make no servants for his work; but they were men of war, and chief of his captains, and captains of his chariots and horsemen."

So their complaint must have been in regard to the heavy taxes, and conscription for military service.

Rehoboam's reply to this demand was, "My father put a heavy yoke upon you, I will put more to your yoke: my father chastised you with whips, but I will chastise you with scorpions" (II Chron. 10:11 KJV).

Obviously, this answer was designed to frighten his questioners and subdue them. Instead, however, the ten tribes of Israel simply walked away from the new king and proclaimed their independence. Intermittent wars between the two kingdoms, and also between each of them and their neighbors, followed. In 722 B.C., Israel was conquered by Assyria, and most of its people were taken into that country where they were assimilated and lost to history as an ethnic people or nation. The northern kingdom was never revived, and the term *Israel* was dropped from the lexicon of contemporary diplomacy.

Judah held out for a while, but as a tributary of Egypt. In 587 B.C., Egypt was driven out by Nebuchadnezzar, who destroyed Jerusalem and carried the cream of Judah captive into Babylonia. So the kingdom of Judah also disappeared. But, unlike the Israelis, the Jews proved unassimilable, and in prayer and song they expressed their longing for Judea. They

5

abhorred life as a subject minority race, bewailed the departed glory of David and Solomon, and sang: "If I forget thee, O Jerusalem, let my right hand forget her cunning."

Shortly after the conquest of Babylonia by Persia, Haman, the "prime minister" who had become angry because a certain Jew named Mordecai would not bow to him, used this longing for Jerusalem and the tenacious adherence of the Jews to their own laws and customs as a basis for recommending to the king that all Jews be killed because "their laws are diverse from all people; neither keep they the king's laws" (Esth. 3:8 KJV). But the day was saved by Mordecai's niece, Esther or Hadassah, who had become King Ahasuerus' queen. And instead of the Jews being killed, Haman himself, and his ten sons, and 75,000 other Persians were killed by the Jews (Esth. 9 KJV) and thousands of Persians adopted Judaism for fear of the Jews.[1] This episode, which the Jews still celebrate as Purim, was the first great religious conflict between them and the gentile world outside of Palestine.

After Babylon was subjugated by Persia, the Emperor Cyrus gave the Jews permission to return to Jerusalem and to rebuild Solomon's temple, which had been destroyed by the Babylonians.

Ezra, the priest who recorded the story, says that 42,360 Jews with 7,337 servants returned and started the rebuilding program.[1] But the neighbors stopped them. They wrote the Great King to the effect that if the wall of Jerusalem and the temple are rebuilt, the Jews would soon rebel and cease to pay taxes. Eventually, however, the Jews prevailed and the building job was completed. Persian rule was tolerant, and the Jews were allowed to practice their religious rituals and customs, but as tributaries of Persia.

This situation continued until the conquest of the Persian

---

1. The Jews seem to have prospered in Babylon as exiles, judging by the number of servants they brought home with them—one for every six persons.

empire by Alexander the Great. Greek rule then replaced that of Persia.

The people of Syria and Palestine accepted the Greek culture, which was destined to become the basis of European civilization. But the Jews, who had been leading a separate existence apart from their neighbors, resisted the new order. When the Greek ruler of Syria, Epiphanes, attempted to suppress Judaism, the priests of Yahweh led a rebellion, which, largely due to the fact that the Greeks were busy fighting the Persians, met with considerable success.

The Maccabees, after freeing Judea, were encouraged to spread their rule over a large area around it. In some instances, to make their rule safe, they followed the Greek policy against which they had rebelled, and forced the conquered population to accept their own religion.

But their empire did not last long. It was brought to an end in 63 B.C. when the Roman legions under Pompey occupied Syria and Palestine. The Romans installed Antipater, a half-Arab Indumean leader, as king in Jerusalem and permitted the Jews a measure of religious and political freedom. King Herod the Great, a successor of Antipater, rebuilt the Jewish temple which had been greatly damaged during the war. There was a respite from wars for a time—a short time, for soon the "stiff-necked" people rose in revolt. The result was to be expected.

In the year A.D. 70, Jerusalem was burned, and a number of Jewish leaders were removed to Rome to prevent another uprising.

The Diaspora—the dispersion of the Jews—now became a fact. A large number of the Jews taken to Babylonia by Nebuchadnezzar failed to return to Judea when Cyrus granted them permission to do so. And a considerable number of Jews were in Egypt, some having been taken there as prisoners of war and some having voluntarily migrated there to share in the prosperity of Alexandria, the seaport city built by Alexander. The Septuagint version of the Old Testament was

7

produced by the Jews of Alexandria, not by those in Jerusalem.

Despite their crushing defeat, the Jews soon renewed their resistance. Scarcely half a century later, they staged another rebellion. This time the Romans acted decisively, hoping to end "the Jewish question" once and for all. Titus not only crushed their fighting force but also razed Jerusalem completely, including the temple. A new city was later built on the historic site, but the Romans called it "Aelia Capitolina," thinking that this would erase the memory of Jerusalem from the Jewish mind. They also issued a decree barring the Jews from this new city.

The name "Aelia Capitolina" was still attached to this city when Emperor Constantine became a Christian in the fourth century A.D. The bar against Jews in the now Christian city, which included those who had become Christians, remained in force until it was removed by the Muslims centuries later.

Rome's action ended the concentration of Jews in Jerusalem and Judea and eliminated the possibility of any further violent uprising there. But it did not solve "the Jewish question," as the Romans had hoped.

Even prior to the destruction of Jerusalem and while chafing under Roman rule, the Jews became involved in a more serious conflict, a conflict which has continued to this day. This is the conflict between them and Christianity.

It was to escape from this old and continuing conflict that Theodor Herzl and his followers plunged the Jews into war with the Arab and Islamic worlds which theretofore had been friendly toward them. And the pity of it is that the new conflict, as might have been expected, has been fanning the flames of the old one instead of extinguishing them. It has raised the spector of double loyalty even in the countries in which the Jews had enjoyed full freedom and equality.

The Bible says that Jesus was born a Jew. But his teachings were irreconcilable with the current teachings of the Jews and struck at their very foundations. He rejected racial exclusive-

8

ness practiced by the Jews, especially since their return from Babylonia, when under order of the priest Ezra they "put away all strange wives, and such as born of them." He scorned the idea of a super or holy race. He told his audiences to seek the Kingdom of Heaven instead of the restoration of the Jewish kingdom in Jerusalem. He thus infuriated the nationalistic elements among the Jews, especially the priests.

These priests and the members of the Sanhedrin had heard similar challenges to their teachings from their neighbors and from their masters, the Greeks and the Romans. But they were able to neutralize them easily by simply pointing out that they were "foreign" ideas and not fit for the children of Judah. They could not say that about Jesus, who spoke as a Jew and often quoted the Torah and the prophets. The Nazarene's teachings were more dangerous than the Roman legions.

So they tried to eliminate him and suppress his teachings. After the crucifixion they hunted down his followers. But these followers, mostly Jewish, soon won out, and Christianity, despite persecution by both Jews and Romans—or perhaps because of such persecution—continued to spread. Early in the fourth century, the Emperor Constantine was converted, and Christianity became the national religion of the Roman Empire, including the Near East. Christians, previously persecuted by the Jews, now took the offensive and became persecutors.

Christianity as practiced by the alleged followers of the Prince of Peace, who exhorted people to be humble, to love their neighbors, and to turn the other cheek, did not bring religious peace to Europe. Certainly not to the Jews there. The Jews, the descendants of Judah and Jacob as well as the converts to Judaism, to this day have been suffering at the hands of the so-called Christians.

There is no need to recount the gruesome tales of the persecution of Jews in Europe; their expulsion from England in the thirteenth century, from France in the fourteenth century, and from Spain and its possessions—including Sardinia, Sicily and Naples—in 1492. These are well known to the reader. Nor is there any need to go into details of the Russian pogroms or of Hitler's concentration camps and gas chambers which took place in our own time. But we should point out that it was persecution of Jews by Christians in Europe which gave birth to the Zionist movement and that Adolph Hitler, the greatest single enemy of the Jews in modern times, made the greatest contribution to the success of this movement. Without Hitler and his gas chambers, the political, scientific, and economic elite of the state of present day Israel would still be going about their business in Germany today, as their six million coreligionists are doing in America.

From time to time Jewish leaders and others tried to find a solution to the "Jewish question." Many thought that emancipation—freedom and equal rights for the Jews in their native countries—was the best remedy and labored to achieve this goal. Aided by the new enlightenment of the nineteenth and twentieth centuries, they achieved considerable success. The French revolution, with its slogans of liberty and equality, gave the emancipation movement a great impetus. For a time, the solution seemed to be at hand.

But the Zionists, the followers of Hess and Theodor Herzel, rejected emancipation, insisting on a separate life as Jews. And as we have stated, Hitler came to their aid. He gave Zionism the *raison d'être* hitherto lacking. When Israel was born, post-Hitler West Germany gave her over a billion dollars in "reparations," which enabled her to stand on her feet. Hitler also won the sympathy of the American people for Zionism.

And so the Christian-Jewish conflict in Europe gave birth to Zionism and the Arab-Jewish conflict. Zionist leaders searched among the colonial-minded European nations for support and finally succeeded in inducing Great Britain, the leading colonial power of the time, to sponsor their movement and fight for it.

The doors of Palestine were opened to Jewish immigration by the military might of Christian Britain, with the approval of other Christian nations. The resolution of the United Nations to partition Palestine and create a Jewish state in it was approved by Christian nations only. Of course, these nations knew full well that the creation of a Jewish state in the heart of the Arab world would unquestionably start a war between the two hitherto friendly peoples. And when war did come, the Christian nations fanned its flames and smilingly said "a plague upon both your houses."

II

The Expanding War: "From a Little Acorn"

The Arab-Zionist war started in the closing days of the last century when the Zionist Organization was formed and its leaders began to seek support for large-scale Jewish colonization of Palestine. But since the antagonists were far apart, there was no physical encounter. Even when some Jews began to come and settle in Palestine, the Arabs did not object—not seriously, anyway. Some men, like Nejib Nassar, editor of the weekly newspaper *Al-Carmel*, did repeatedly warn of the danger ahead. But how could a few hundred, or a few thousand, Jewish families constitute a danger to Palestine or to the Arab world?

Then, in 1914, came the First World War. During the dark days of that war when German victory seemed certain, the alert Zionists made a deal with the British government and obtained the Balfour Declaration, which promised British aid in creating a Jewish "national home" in Palestine.

The Arabs protested but were quickly reassured by London. Nevertheless this document, which was only a letter from the British foreign minister to Baron Rothschild, made Britain a party to the Arab-Zionist conflict and compelled her to maintain a huge army there for thirty years. So the conflict now included a great world power. And soon this great power,

12

after occupying Palestine and opening wide its gates to Jewish immigrants, was shooting down the Arabs who resisted its policy.

Under the protection of British guns, the Jewish population of the country was increased from fifty-five thousand in 1918 to six hundred and fifty thousand in 1947 and had a British-equipped and British-trained army numbering sixty thousand to one hundred thousand.

In 1947 the British decided to give up the mandate over Palestine entrusted to them by the League of Nations. They asked the United Nations, as the League's successor, to decide the future of Palestine.

The fledgling world peace organization, under pressure by the United States, adopted a resoltuion that called for the creation of a Jewish state in parts of Palestine. The Arabs rejected this plan and called for a united and independent Palestine. The Jews who, despite three decades of unrestricted immigration, were still outnumbered by the Arabs two to one insisted on partition.

Fighting erupted. The Arabs, unorganized and having been previously disarmed, could not defend themselves against the well-armed and well-trained Jewish forces. As a result, some three hundred thousand Arabs were driven into Jordan, Syria, and Lebanon, creating problems for those states.

On May 15, 1948, the date set by the British for giving up the mandate and on which the Jews in Palestine declared the formation of the state of Israel, the Arab states around Palestine sent troops to aid the Palestinians. The conflict heretofore between the Palestinians and the Jewish settlers had now become one between the Arab world and world Jewry that backed Israel to the hilt.

The United Nations arranged an armistice in February 1949. In May 1950 the United States, Great Britain, and France issued a joint declaration in which they threatened intervention in case an attempt is made to change the frontiers of any state in the area by force. This solemn warning by the

13

great Western powers was said to be intended to promote peace and stability. It did that, and it also confirmed Israel in the territory it then occupied, which was 40 percent larger than the area allotted to her by the United Nations' partition resolution.

So the three great Western powers became involved in the conflict.

A few Palestinian refugees calling themselves *fedayeen*, i.e., persons willing to die for the cause, began to make incursions across the armistice line into the Negeb for sabotage purposes. Israel retaliated by attacking the Egyptian forces in Gaza.

Finding his army unequipped to deter or repel these attacks, and denied weapons by the Western powers, President Nasser of Egypt made a deal for the purchase of some hardware from Czechoslovakia, and the Communist bloc got into the act. The camel, or rather the bear, got his nose into the Arab's tent.

To punish Nasser for this "impudence," Washington and London canceled an offer of a loan to start work on the Aswan High Dam. The Soviet Union jumped at the opportunity to finance and build the dam. So the bear got his head and neck in the Arab's tent.

When Israel, France, and Britain attacked Egypt on October 29, 1956, the Kremlin quickly sent threatening notes to the three invaders and followed this by rearming Egypt, thus establishing itself as the friend of the Arabs.

A decade later came the Six Day War and the defeat of the Arabs. Soviet Prime Minister Alexsei N. Kosygin himself came to the U.N. to fight for the Arab cause while Soviet planes and ships poured arms into Egypt and Syria. The bear was now totally in. At the same time the United States stood solidly behind Israel. Her spokesman there at the time was Ambassador Arthur Goldberg, himself a Zionist Jew. American war jets poured into Israel, which previously had been receiving arms through England, France, and Germany. Now the United States openly became the supplier of her weapons.

The war between Israel and the Arabs thus became one between the United States and the Soviet Union, albeit by proxy and not directly.

Russia and her satellites, with the exception of Romania, severed diplomatic relations with Israel. Egypt and five other Arab states severed diplomatic relations with the United States.

At this writing, the United States is still backing Israel with money and arms, but the rest of the world has taken a stand against her. Even England and France have modified their attitude toward Israel and have voted against her at the U.N. more than once since 1967. Indeed, when the 1967 war started, France quickly embargoed fifty jets previously ordered by Israel, because President DeGaulle held that Israel was the aggressor in this war.

The Soviet Union remains on the Arab side despite President Sadat's expulsion of the Russian military advisers from Egypt in July 1972. And notwithstanding the thaw achieved at the Moscow and Washington summit meetings between former President Richard M. Nixon and Communist Party General Secretary Leonid I. Brezhnev, the two great powers remain deeply involved in the conflict and on opposite sides.

When the October 1973 war started and news of the Egyptian success in crossing the Suez Canal reached Secretary of State Henry A. Kissinger, units of the United States fleet were immediately ordered to the Eastern Mediterranean and an airlift of arms to Tel Aviv—$2.2 billion worth—was mounted. Moreover, the United States armed forces were alerted for global war. Russia, of course, poured quantities of arms into Egypt and Syria and backed them politically.

The lines of battle remain drawn. The United States continues to pour arms and dollars into Israel. The Soviet Union, although somewhat cool toward Egypt since President Sadat developed such close relations with Henry Kissinger, has continued to back the Arab cause.

Unless a political settlement is made soon, an explosion seems inevitable, and the two superpowers are likely to be sucked into it whether they will it or not.

III

The Third Jewish Invasion of Palestine

According to the Old Testament, the first Hebrew invasion of Palestine took place from the East across the Jordan River. It is also recorded that the Hebrew tribes—twelve in number—including the tribe of Judah, entered together under one commander, Joshua.

Historical evidence, however, suggests that these tribes entered the country at different times, perhaps singly, and later banded together and subjugated the Canaanites.

The second invasion, this time by the tribe of Judah alone, also came from the East, under the aegis of Persia which then ruled the region.

The recent invasion, which culminated in the establishment of the state of Israel, took place from the west across the Mediterranean Sea.

This new invasion, too, was not accomplished by a frontal attack upon the country's inhabitants but by a slow process of *immigration* that took half a century for the invaders to become strong enough to achieve their goal of dispossessing the indigenous population.

The third invasion took place under the protection of imperial Britain which at one time had some one hundred thousand troops stationed there to protect the Jewish immigrants and help them prepare to take over the country. When Britain was eventually forced to give up its empire and the Jewish immigrants had become strong enough militarily to vanquish the Palestinians, Great Britain decided to withdraw from Palestine.

Then the United States, which had become the world's greatest power, rushed in with massive political, financial, and military aid which has made the state proclaimed in 1948 by the six hundred thousand new immigrants the strongest military power in the area. Indeed, these immigrants, numbering only two million five hundred thousand in 1967, had a military machine that in six days defeated Egypt, Jordan, and Syria, occupied large areas of their territories, and has held them in defiance of the whole Arab world and of the United Nations also, thanks to continuous strong backing by the United States.

The story of this new invasion and its success is interesting and worth following from the beginning.

Jewish immigration to Palestine began in the 1880's before the formation of the Zionist Organization. These early immigrants were mainly people who sought a refuge from Russian and Polish oppression. They were not opposed by the Palestinians. However, when Theodor Herzl, the founder of the Zionist Organization, asked Constantinople, which then ruled Palestine, for permission to colonize the country by Jews and turn it into a Jewish state, they objected vigoriously enough to cause the sultan to reject Herzl's petition despite the great rewards offered him.

Sultan Abdul Hamid's action reassured the Palestinians and all the Arabs around them. Herzl's Jewish state project was dead, or so they thought. The arrival of a few more Jewish immigrants did not seem to constitute a threat.

Even the arrival in Sajara, Galilee, in 1906 of that arch Zionist who is credited with the building of Israel, David Gren, later known as David Ben-Gurion, did not stir them. They did not know what he had up his sleeve.

18

The Zionists, rebuffed by Constantinople, sought the support of Berlin, which had begun to enjoy some influence among the Turks. But Kaiser Wilhelm's government showed no desire to rush to their support.

Then came the First World War and the great German victories on both the Western and Eastern fronts. The Russian armies were melting, and defeat stared England and France in the face.

Israel's first president, Russian-born Chaim Weizmann, a scientist then living in London, developed a formula for producing TNT cheaply. He presented this formula to the British government, won its gratitude and also ready access to Prime Minister David Lloyd George's ear. He and Baron Walter Rothschild, of the famous European financial family, proposed that Britain help the Zionist Organization establish a Jewish state in Palestine, which London did not then possess or rule. Their proposal was strongly supported by Sir Herbert Samuel, a Zionist Jew who was a member of the war cabinet, and who later became Great Britain's first high commissioner in Palestine.

A Jewish state in Palestine, the Zionist advocates said, would be an effective guardian of Britain's interests in the Middle East, especially the Suez Canal, its lifeline to India. It would also keep out France, her perennial rival, which had been claiming Syria—including Lebanon and Palestine—as her exclusive sphere of influence.[2] (France later was granted a mandate by the League of Nations over Syria and Lebanon, while Britain was given the mandate over Iraq, Trans Jordan, and Palestine.) In addition, the Zionist spokesmen assured His

---

2. Oddly enough, prior advocates of a Jewish state had suggested that France sponsor their project and establish herself astride the Suez Canal, which France had encouraged and Britain had opposed building. France, they said, would then have a safe route to India and China with their rich trade. Ironically, too, the creation of Israel and its war against the Arabs in 1956 and 1967 caused the closure of this important canal.

Majesty's government that they would, through Jewish influence in the United States—particularly that of Justice Louis Brandeis, President Wilson's close friend and appointee to the United States Supreme Court—induce America to enter the war on England's side.[3] England agreed. Prime Minister David Lloyd George wrote later that the Zionists had promised to rally world Jewry to the support of England.

In November 1916, Woodrow Wilson was reelected president of the United States. The oft-repeated slogan during his election campaign was, "He kept us out of war." But on April 6, 1917, scarcely a month after his second inauguration, he asked the Congress of the United States to declare war on Germany. The Congress did.

The Zionists, having fulfilled their part of the bargain, asked London to acknowledge its obligation publicly and in writing.

Then began the difficult task of complying with Zionist demands without offending the anti-Zionist Jews, headed by Edwin Montagu, who attacked the proposal as anti-Semitic, or angering the Arabs with whom London had made a treaty that promised them aid in obtaining independence in return for joining the war against the Turks. Arab troops were already fighting the now common enemy, Turkey, which was allied with Germany.

Turkey's defeat and its elimination from the war would have a great military, political, and psychological impact on the war and its aftermath. And so said the Allies military representatives in a memorandum submitted to the Supreme War Council in January 1918, eight months after the entry of the United States into the war.[4] Could they afford to Alienate the Arabs?

---

3. See article by S. Landman, then Secretary of the Zionist Organization, in the *Jewish Chronicle*, December 20, 1935. See also what Mr. Landman says in his book *Great Britain, the Jews, and Palestine* about America's entry into World War I and its connection with the rise of Hitlerism in Germany.

4. *War Memoirs of David Lloyd George,* 1917-1918.

The Zionists submitted several drafts that went into details reciting what the British government was to do for them. These drafts were found too strong and embarrassing and were rejected.

Finally, on November 2, 1917, after securing the consent of the United States and France, the following short and purposely vague letter was addressed by Foreign Minister Arthur J. Balfour to Baron Walter Rothschild:

> I have much pleasure in conveying to you, on behalf of His Majesty's Government, the following declaration of sympathy with Jewish Zionist aspirations which has been submitted to, and approved by, the cabinet.
>
> His Majesty's Government view with favour the establishment in Palestine of a national home for the Jewish people, and will use their best endeavours to facilitate the achievement of this object, it being clearly understood that nothing shall be done which may prejudice the civil and religious rights of existing non-Jewish communities in Palestine, or the rights and political status enjoyed by Jews in any other country.

It will be noted that this letter was addressed to a private citizen and not to the head of, or an official of, a state. Hence it could not be called a treaty and so had no validity in international law. No consideration was stated for Britain's very important undertaking which proved to be very costly. Moreover, Britain's promise was to help the Zionists establish a national home in a territory that belonged to and was inhabited by another people, the Palestinian Christian and Moslem Arabs, most of whom had been there since time immemorial. It was a promise by A to give C the home of his friend and ally B. Obviously it was an illegal and immoral undertaking.

Yet Zionist propaganda gave it a sacrosanct character and made it appear as sacred as Yahweh's promise to Abraham. They called it the "Balfour Declaration" to clothe it with importance. They publicized it so widely that it became almost as well known as the Bible. In their writings and debates, it was presented as a warranty title deed to the farmlands, towns, and villages of Palestine.

But they took care not to mention the proviso in this document that guaranteed the rights of the Arabs, who were referred to as "the non-Jewish communities" in the country, thus making them look like an insignificant entity, although they constituted more than 90 percent of the population.

Nor did the Zionists, or the British for that matter, ever give a clear definition of the vague term *national home*, which London obligated itself to help create for the Jews in Palestine.

In the early days, Zionist leaders tried to allay Arab fears by assuring them that the coming of the Jews would not hurt them and that, on the contrary, it would help raise their standard of living.

In an interview with the *Times* of London on March 22, 1922, Dr. Chaim Weizmann, then head of the World Zionist Organization, said: "We do not aspire to found a state. What we want is a country in which all nations and all creeds shall have equal rights and equal tolerance."

This was a few months before the League of Nations granted Britain the mandate over Palestine. As soon as the mandate was approved, Dr. Weizmann and his followers went to work. Twenty-six years later, a Jewish state was established and most of the Moslem and Christian inhabitants of Palestine were forced out. They have not been permitted to return home.

Dr. Weizmann became the first president of the new state, and in his capacity as president, he looked on with satisfaction while Jewish troops and terrorist organizations cleared the land of its Moslem and Christian inhabitants. Arab homes and Arab lands were taken over by the new Jewish immigrants who flooded the country following the proclamation of the establishment of Israel. Over one hundred villages were completely destroyed to prevent the return of their inhabitants.

Dr. Weizmann did condemn the Irgun Zvai Leumi attack on the village of Deir Yasin and assured the survivors who had been driven out that their property would be protected until they came back home. But that is as far as he went.

The British repeatedly assured the Arabs that their rights and position would be scrupulously protected. Lord Balfour himself, the author of the Balfour Declaration, was very eloquent in assuring them that his statement did not mean that a Jewish state would be permitted in Palestine. Indeed, he felt rather indignant when the question was raised. In a speech in the House of Lords on March 23, 1922, the day following Weizmann's interview with the *Times*, his Lordship said:

It is surely a very poor compliment to the British Government, to the Governor of Palestine appointed by the British Government, to the Mandates Commission under the League of Nations, whose business it is to see that the spirit as well as the letter of the Mandates is carried out, and beyond them to the Council of the League of Nations, to suppose that all these bodies will so violate every pledge that they have ever given, and every principle to which they have ever subscribed, as to use the power given them by the Peace Treaty to enable one section of the community of Palestine to oppress and dominate any other. . . . I cannot imagine any political interests exercised under greater safeguards than the political interests of the Arab population of Palestine. Every act of government will be jealously watched. The Zionist Organization has no attribution of political powers. If it uses or usurps political powers it is an act of usurpation. Whatever else may happen in Palestine, of this I am very confident, that under British Government no form of tyranny, racial or religious, will be permitted. (Document provided by H.M. Government on August 31, 1947, to the U.N. Special Committee on Palestine.)

It must be said that the British administration in Palestine did not expressly permit or authorize the creation of a Jewish state. The idea of partitioning the country between the Jews and the Arabs was considered once but was quickly dropped because of Arab opposition. As we have seen, however, when the British left in 1948, the Arabs were helpless. They had been disarmed, but the Jews were armed and trained and the Jewish Agency had a well-organized "shadow government" in Palestine ready to take over at short notice.

Strangely, Zionist and Israeli spokesmen no longer mention the Balfour Declaration or the terms of the mandate—and for a good reason. Their application today would require the dismantling of the state of Israel, the removal of more than two million Jews from the country, and the repatriation of the Palestinians who lost their homes since Israel was created.

Ironically, Lord Balfour was himself anti-Semitic. As prime minister before World War I, he supported legislation to limit Jewish immigration into his country.

England occupied Palestine and, under the mandate of the League of Nations, ruled it for thirty years and made it possible for the Zionists to establish in it not a national home but a Jewish state. Eighty percent of the Arab population of the country were killed or driven out.

Of course, when news of the Balfour letter reached the Arabs, they protested. But Britain told them not to worry. Jewish immigration will not be so large as to hurt the people of Palestine. After all, the Balfour letter itself guarantees their rights. (For a detailed study of the history of Palestine and Arab-British relations, see my book *Palestine Dilemma* [Washington, D.C.: 1948]).

Palestine was occupied by a British army under General Allenby who told the people that he had come to liberate them from Turkish rule. As a further assurance to them, Great Britain and France on November 7, 1918, a year after the Balfour letter, issued a joint declaration in which they said that their war aims in the Near East were "the complete and final liberation of the peoples who have for so long been oppressed by the Turks, and the setting up of national governments and administrations that shall derive their authority from the . . . indigenous populations." The declaration pledged help in setting up such national governments and promised economic aid.

In 1922 the League of Nations approved a mandate charging Britain to lead Palestine toward independence, but it also incorporated the provisions of the Balfour Declaration—verbatim. So the British remained in Palestine, and Jewish immigrants came into the country without restrictions, despite the continuous protests of its Arab population and even their violent demonstrations.

In 1924, the United States, alarmed at the stream of Jewish immigrants from eastern Europe, enacted the quota immigration law. This law helped the Zionists to recruit immigrants for Palestine. And for a while Jewish immigration boomed. However, beginning in 1927, there was a sharp decrease. Only 2,713 persons came to the country that year as compared to 13,081 in 1926. Moreover, 5,071 Jews left during that year. The year 1928 also was bad for the Zionists. In that year 2,178 came to live in Palestine while an almost equal number—2,168—left it. Apparently the Jews did not cherish the harsh life offered them in the land of "milk and honey." The Arabs seemed reassured.

But then Adolf Hitler came into power in Germany and started his war against the peace treaty and the Jews. The Germans, resenting the oppressive burdens saddled upon them by the peace treaty and believing that the Jews had influenced the United States to enter the war against them, applauded his anti-Semitic harangues. The flight of Jews began. Unable to enter their dream country—the United States—the Jews of Germany, Poland, and Austria accepted Zionist offers of aid to send them to Palestine. The number of those who responded to Zionist appeals in 1933 was 30,327. In

1934 it rose to 42,359. In 1935 it jumped to 61,541.

The Arabs of Palestine became alarmed. Conquest through immigration stared them in the face. They renewed their struggle but to no avail. The Jews continued to pour in under the protection of British banonets and tanks.

Having been disarmed by the British, and confronted by a large British army plus the important *Haganah*—the Jewish "defense" army created by Ben-Gurion—the Arabs borrowed from Ghandi's peaceful resistance methods. They declared a general strike in 1936 which paralyzed the country for over six months.

As Jews continued to arrive in Palestine, Arab demonstrations and even violence continued to break out from time to time with heavy losses to Arabs, Jews, and British. More troops were brought in, but the Arabs continued to protest.

Hitler's policies soon convinced the British authorities that despite the Munich agreement war with him was inevitable. They started to put their house in order and to secure their flanks. Realizing that Arab goodwill was essential to them, His Majesty's Government now recalled, belatedly, that both the Balfour Declaration and the mandate enjoined them to protect Arab rights and position and that the mandate obligated them to lead the country toward self-government. They stated that unlimited Jewish immigration now constituted a threat to the Arabs and therefore should be controlled.

In a white paper issued in May 1939, London talked of self-government in which Jews and Arabs would participate "when the country is ready for it" but not now. In the meantime, this paper said, Palestinians—Arabs and Jews—will be invited to become department heads (with British advisers to run them) to prepare the country for self-government.

As to immigration, the paper proposed to admit at once twenty-five thousand Jews and then limit immigration visas to fifteen hundred a month for five years. The white paper also said, "After the period of five years no further Jewish immigration will be permitted unless the Arabs of Palestine are prepared to acquiesce in it."

The Zionists rose up in arms. In protest against the new immigration policy, they blew up the *SS.Patria* in 1940 in the port of Haifa. Two hundred and sixty-eight Jewish lives were lost. Jewish terrorist organizations, such as the Stern Gang and the Irgun Zvai Leumi, took to the field against their erstwhile protectors. The British resident minister in the Middle East, Lord Moyne, was assassinated in 1944. The King David Hotel at Jerusalem, which housed the British army headquarters and the secretariat of the Palestine government, was blown up in 1946 with heavy loss of life—British, Arab, and Jewish. Bridges, railroads, etc. were blown up.

Letter bombs were sent to British officials in London and elsewhere. Sabotage became so widespread that the British found it necessary to evacuate their families for safety. A boycott of British products was also carried out by Jews everywhere. The smuggling of Jews into Palestine became big business.

The fact that the British were then fighting Jewry's arch enemy did not seem to matter.

IV

Exit Britain; Enter the United States

President Franklin D. Roosevelt repeatedly expressed sympathy with the Zionists' aims. But he took no positive action to help them. And when Representative (Jewish Zionist) Sol Bloom introduced a resolution in the U.S. House of Representatives in April 1944, calling upon the United States to take measures to open Palestine to the "free entry of Jews," War Secretary Stimson prevailed upon him to withdraw it, lest it inflame the Arabs whose goodwill and support were needed. Secretary Stimson's objections to this resolution were later withdrawn when the war situation improved and Arab goodwill was no longer crucial.

At a meeting with King Abdul-Aziz, President Roosevelt promised orally and later, on April 5, 1945, wrote him that "it was America's settled policy that no decision be taken with respect to the basic situation in that country (Palestine) without full consultation with both Arabs and Jews."

A short time later, he said, "A Zionist state in Palestine can only be installed and maintained by force and we should not be a party to it."

Roosevelt's successor, Harry S. Truman, who complained in his memoirs of excessive Zionist pressure and whose complaint was supported by his daughter, Margaret Truman Daniels,[5] succumbed to this pressure and to political exigencies. Moved by sympathy for the Jews found in Hitler's concentration camps, plus his desire to please his friend and former business partner Edward Jacobson (denied by his daughter but amply proved by Jacobson's diary[6]) he ignored President Roosevelt's letter to ibn-Saud, publicly and vigorously backed the Zionist's demands, and pressured London to change the policy of limited immigration. This led Foreign Secretary Bevin to invite the United States to "share the cost of maintaining 90,000 troops in Palestine."[7]

This acrimonious exchange between London and Washington resulted in the appointment of a committee consisting of six Americans and six Britons that was instructed to visit Palestine, study the problem, and submit its recommendations to the two governments. This committee's report, dated April 30, 1946, recommended against unrestricted Jewish immigration but suggested the admission of the one hundred thousand Jews then in European refugee camps who were not wanted by any European nation and who were barred from coming to the United States by our immigration laws. The Arabs, too, objected to dumping them in Palestine. (President Roosevelt had offered to introduce legislation to permit them to come to the United States, but the Zionist leaders insisted that Palestine was the proper place for them.) The committee also recommended the granting of independence to the country after a period of preparation. The Zionists frowned upon this and some other recommendations. The whole report then went into limbo.

---

5. Margaret Truman Daniels, *Harry S Truman.*

6. See *The Diary of Eddie Jacobson* by Joel Levitch and Laurel Flock, the *Washington Post.* May 6, 1973.

7. Daniels, *op. cit.*

V

Palestine at the United Nations

Pressed by Washington, suffering considerable losses at the hands of Jewish terrorists, a worldwide boycott of British products by the Jews (who are an important element in the retail trade), and faced with Arab insistence on the protection of their rights, the British decided to quit Palestine. On April 2, 1947, they notified the United Nations of their decision and asked it to settle the mess they had created. Today, more than a quarter of a century later, the United Nations is still trying, but rather feebly.

Between 1947 and 1974 the problem of Palestine came before the General Assembly 86 times and before the Security Council 133 times. No other problem has taken so much of the United Nations' time. No other problem has cost the United Nations so much money—money to support the Palestinian refugees, the U. N. truce observers, and the peace-keeping ⁺roops. And the mess still has not been settled.

At the time the British began to rule Palestine, its Jewish population was fifty-five thousand. When they dumped the problem into the lap of the United Nations, there were six hundred thousand more Jews in the country. But the Arabs still outnumbered them two to one. There were about

1,250,000 Arabs then. And the Jews still owned less than 6 percent of the land.

The United Nations General Assembly appointed a special committee consisting of representatives of eleven countries to study the problem and report on it. The report of this committee, submitted on August 31, 1947, showed that the members agreed on the basic facts but disagreed on the remedy. A minority recommended independence under a unitary, democratic government. The majority recommended the partition of the country and the creation in it of two independent states, one Arab and one Jewish, and an international administration for Jerusalem and Bethlehem but with continued economic union.

The Jewish state, as it was finally decided, was to have an area of 5,893 square miles. While a large portion of it consisted of the undeveloped Negeb desert, it included the principal fertile plains of the country. The area left for the Arab state was 4,476 square miles. This comprised western Galilee and the hill country once known as Samaria and Judea (now being referred to as the "West Bank" of Jordan) and also a strip of land around Gaza.

On November 29, 1947, the United Nations General Assembly, by Resolution No. 181, after heavy pressure by the United States, adopted this complicated Partition Plan. The vote, 33 in favor, 13 against, and 10 abstaining, was indicative of the mixed feelings and misgivings of the delegates. England was among those abstaining. The Arab states and the Palestinian Arabs opposed it vigorously and demanded independence for Palestine under a democratic government with adequate guarantees for the Jewish minority.

Many delegates questioned the legality of the Partition Plan. But a motion to submit it to the International Court of Justice for decision was blocked. The dilemma of many delegates who, for one reason or another, supported partition was well expressed by Van Langenhove, Foreign Minister of

Belgium, who said, "We are not certain that it is completely just; we doubt whether it is practical; and we are afraid that it involves great risk."[8] Yet he voted for it.

To make certain that all the Jews in the country are included in the territory allocated to the Jewish state, they indulged in a ridiculous process of gerrymandering. After declaring Jerusalem and Bethlehem a *corpus separatum,* they divided the country into six regions and allocated three to each of the proposed states. The three Arab regions had an almost wholly Arab population—seven hundred thousand Arabs and only eight thousand Jews. But these three regions were not connected. If an Arab wished to travel from one region to another, he had to go through one of the Jewish sections at a certain designated crossing point. Likewise, the Jewish state area consisted of three unconnected regions, with crossings at these designated points.

Despite its efforts at gerrymandering, the committee was unable to allocate to the Jewish state a territory with a wholly Jewish population nor even one with a Jewish majority. The Jews were not a majority in any of the then existing political districts of the country. The three regions allocated to it had five thousand more Arabs than Jews. Since it was stipulated that both states must be democratic, it was not feasible to create a Jewish state in this territory.

To overcome this difficulty, the United States delegation proposed that the wholly Arab city of Jaffa—population seventy thousand—be attached to the Arab state. This gave the Jews an overall majority in their three sections, but a very slim one.

The Partition Plan as originally drafted left the Negeb, i.e., the southern part of Palestine which is largely desert, in the hands of the Arabs. The Zionists demanded its inclusion in the proposed Jewish state. This demand was rejected. But after a personal plea by Dr. Chaim Weizmann, President

8. See record of the 124th meeting of the Assembly, p. 1365.

32

Truman acquiesced and ordered the American delegation at the United Nations to support it. So the Negeb, which is about one third of the country, was given to the Jewish state.

The United Nations mediator, Count Folke Bernadotte, recommended that the Arab refugees be repatriated and that Jerusalem and the Negeb remain Arab. He was shot dead by Jewish terrorists on September 17, 1948; his voice was forever silenced.

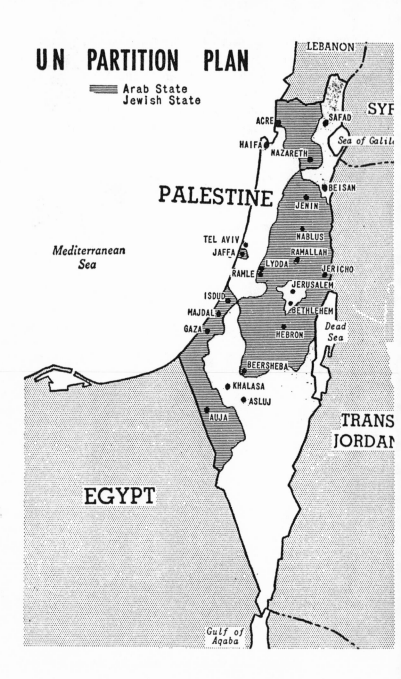

VI

Born in Blood

The Arabs, as stated above, opposed partition. The Zionists worked for it tooth and nail. Although American Zionism's leader, Rabbi Abba Hillel Silver, proudly boasted that the Jews had "forced a decision from the United Nations" for partition, what they got was not exactly what they had aspired for. The Plan did not give them Jerusalem, once Judah's proud capital. Nor did it give them Judea proper. It gave them the rich and level land of the Philistines on the Mediterranean coast and the eastern half of "Galilee of the Gentiles," where many Jewish colonies had been already established. This gave them control of the upper half of the Jordan River and the Lake of Galilee. They also got ancient Edom, the large and as yet undeveloped and sparsely populated Negeb.

Zionist spokesmen had asked the United Nations to add western Galilee and the modern part of Jerusalem to the territory allotted to the Jewish state. The United Nations rejected this request. But the Jews took both, and more, during the fighting that ensued.

The worst feature of the Partition Plan, as far as the Jews were concerned, was the fact that the Arab population of the areas allotted to them was equal to the Jewish population. How can they build a Jewish state in a territory half the population of which was gentile? And the state was required to be democratic in character and obligated by the terms of the Partition Plan to give its Moslem and Christian citizens equal rights with Jews "in civil, political, economic and religious matters; ... freedom of religion, language, speech and publication." (Part I of the Partition Resolution.)

As neither side was happy with the United Nations decision, fighting between Arabs and Jews, which had been in progress on and off for some time, now escalated. And there has been no peace there since.

As it has been stated, the Arabs of Palestine had been disarmed by the British in an effort to maintain peace. They were not organized. They had no trained army or militia and no battle plan. Their leadership was divided—a chronic Arab failing that to this day continues to plague the Arab world.

The Jews, however, were fully prepared for the inevitable showdown. Their leadership was capable and united in its aim. Moreover, they had the Haganah, the army created by David Ben-Gurion a quarter of a century earlier, which now, together with the settlement police and other groups, numbered sixty thousand. This army soon proved to be capable of dealing not only with the Palestinian civilian population but also with the regular armies of the Arab states bordering on Palestine.

The Palestinians tried to obtain arms and to form some defense groups, but what they achieved was "too little and too late."

Units of the Haganah marched at will through the country, occupying town after town and village after village, while the Irgun and Stern Gang, the terrorist organizations that had been inflicting heavy losses on the British, now turned their full fury on the Arabs, causing them to flee in panic. The massacre of the inhabitants of Deir Yassin on April 9, 1948, who had decided not to take part in the fighting because they were surrounded by Jewish settlements but dared to ignore the orders of Menachem Begin, then leader of the Irgun and later head of the Herut party and a member of the government, to

36

evacuate their village, caused thousands to flee upon hearing of the approach of the Jewish forces.

Jacques de Reynier of the International Red Cross counted 254 corpses, mostly women and children. One hundred and fifty of these corpses were found in a cistern, apparently thrown there to cover up, in part at least, the enormity of the crime.

President Truman and Dr. Weizmann, who was in Washington at the time, publicly condemned this Jewish terrorist action. Dr. Weizmann also assured the survivors that their property would be protected until they return. But they have not been allowed to return yet.

Mr. Begin was shortly thereafter given a hero's welcome in New York, and the attack on Deir Yassin, because it accelerated the flight of the Arabs, became known as "the miracle of Deir Yassin."

Deir Yassin, which was to be part of the Jerusalem enclave, is no more. It was razed to the ground and a Jewish settlement—Kfar Sha'ul—was built there.

The Jewish Agency and later the government of Israel tried to disclaim responsibility for this outrageous crime on the ground that the Irgun was not an official organization, but they accepted its fruits and later paid pensions to the members of the Irgun as war veterans.

According to Margaret Truman Daniels, her father wrote Eleanor Roosevelt on August 23, 1947, as follows:

> The action of some of our United States Zionists will eventually prejudice everyone against what they are trying to get done. I fear very much that the Jews are like all underdogs. When they get on top they are just as intolerant and as cruel as the people were to them when they were underneath. I regret this situation very much because my sympathy has always been on their side.[9]

---

9. Daniels, *op. cit.*

Mr. Truman, besides being a good politician, proved to be a good prophet.

The governments of the Arab states looked on, expressed their sorrow for the plight of the Palestinians, and assured them that they would come to their rescue as soon as British rule was ended. Understandably, they did not dare fight the British and the Jews at the same time.

The Partition Resolution stated that the British would withdraw from Palestine gradually, but the country might remain under their control until August 1, 1948, and that the Jewish and the Arab states shall come into being two months after the British evacuation but not later than October 1, 1948. It also provided that a five-member commission would be established to administer the country with the help of provisional councils of government until the new regimes begin to function. The British announced the termination of the mandate as of May 15.

The Jews, who for many years had had a shadow government in Palestine, set up by the Jewish Agency, saw no need to wait. They declared their independence and the formation of a Jewish state on May 14, 1948, under the name of "Israel." They did not call it "the Jewish State," as the founder of Zionism, Theodor Herzl, had called it. And they could not call it "Judea," as the ancient kingdom of Judah was called, because that territory was to remain Arab. They chose the name "Israel" apparently because of the word's spiritual connotation among Christians. As you know, the Christian church is called the "New Israel."

Of course, "Israel" was the name of the kingdom of the ten Hebrew tribes whose capital was Samaria and who often fought Judah. Those tribes had been assimilated in Assyria and became known as "the lost ten tribes" of Israel. They are not here to contest the usurpation of their name by their former enemy, Judah.

President Truman wrote in his memoirs, *Years of Trial and Error,* that the U. N. was subjected to very heavy pressure by the Zionists. He also wrote: "The White House was subjected to a constant barrage. I do not think I ever had as much pressure and propaganda aimed at the White House as I did in this instance. The persistence of a few extreme Zionist leaders—activated by political motives disturbed and annoyed me."

Evidently the president of the United States could not resist this pressure. According to him, the new state was recognized by him with unprecedented speed—"exactly eleven minutes after Israel had been proclaimed as a state."

The president did this despite the fact that he had affirmed President Roosevelt's policy on Palestine as outlined in the letter to King ibn-Saud early in 1945 in which F.D.R. said that America would not take any action on Palestine without consulting both the Arabs and the Jews. Truman had written the prime minister of Egypt, Nukrashy Pasha, and other Arab leaders, "It was my position that the principle of self-determination required that Arabs as well as Jews be consulted."

In his memoirs, he tried to explain away his reneging on his promises to the Arabs by saying, "To assure the Arabs that they would be consulted was by no means inconsistent with my generally sympathetic attitude toward Jewish aspirations."

President Truman, with his usual candor, told a meeting of American ambassadors that his policy on Palestine was influenced in part by the absence of Arabs in the United States.

Truman's speed in recognizing Israel took the U. S. delegation at the U. N. and even the Zionists by surprise. A U. S. delegate was speaking in support of U. N. trusteeship over Palestine when Mr. Truman's action was announced.

The U.S.S.R., which for reasons of its own had voted for the Partition Plan, quickly followed Washington's lead and extended recognition to the prematurely born and still unrecognizable infant. The Kremlin hoped that trouble in the Middle East, coveted by Russia for generations, could open a door in this highly strategic region for the Czars' successors. It soon did.

Noisily and with much fanfare, the Arab armies moved against Israel, only to become the butt of jokes in New York and elsewhere.

According to General John Bagot Glubb, the total Arab forces numbered only 21,500. The Jewish forces then exceeded 60,000.

The Trans-Jordan army marched westward as far as Ramleh and Lydda but soon retreated and allowed the Israelis to occupy the two towns along with the Lydda airport, which they began to use for the importation of arms from the Communist bloc in violation of an embargo imposed by the United Nations. The Egyptian forces marched north along the coast of the Mediterranean but were stopped at Gaza. Defective hand grenades that exploded prematurely in the hands of the soldiers contributed to their difficulties. The small Syrian force that crossed the border of Palestine soon retreated when the Haganah turned on it.

Newly independent Syria was then just starting to build and equip an army. A shipment of weapons purchased in Europe for this army was hijacked on the high seas by the Jews.

An Iraqi contingent, a well-equipped one, reached Nablus and struck camp there. It never engaged the enemy. It returned home without firing a shot. "No orders," said one officer when asked to advance and save Haifa.

It has been reliably reported that when the Jews in Haifa learned of the strength of this Iraqi army, they decided not to fight but rather negotiate the surrender of the city. But they did not have to surrender. The Iraqis did not attack.

Mahmoud Roussan, a Jordanian major whose battalion fought the Jews in Jerusalem, told this writer that the Arab legion had occupied most of new Jerusalem when his superior officer, a Briton, ordered him to withdraw and threatened to shoot him if he disobeyed.

The United Nations appointed Count Folke Bernadotte of Sweden as mediator to arrange for ending the fighting and restoring peace and order. As we have seen, he and a member of his staff, French Colonel Serot, were assassinated by Jews on September 17 when it became known that his ideas did not coincide with those of the Jewish leaders. His assistant, Ralph Bunche of the United States, took over the difficult job. Dr. Bunche worked hard and persistently, and finally, after a couple of cease fires, he succeeded in bringing about an armistice in February 1949.

When this armistice was signed, the Jews were in control of over two thousand square miles of territory more than had been allotted to them. Two thousand square miles are important considering that Palestine's total area is barely ten thousand square miles. They had taken all of Western Galilee, one of the three sections that were to form the Arab state, and parts of the other two sections. In addition, they had taken the new part of Jerusalem that adjoins the western wall of the old city. This gave them a solid piece of territory, so they no longer had to pass through Arab land when going from one section to another of the three sections allotted to them by the United Nations.

More important, they had driven out over nine hundred thousand Arabs from the territory they occupied and made it easier for them to form a truly Jewish state.

Less than two hundred thousand Arabs were permitted to remain in the occupied territory to become "hewers of wood and drawers of water." The farmers, having lost their fields, became common laborers.

During the fighting, the Egyptian army reached Gaza and was still there when the armistice took effect. It was briefly driven out in 1956. In 1967 it was driven back all the way to the west bank of the Suez Canal.

The Jordanian army held Hebron, Bethlehem, Old Jeru-

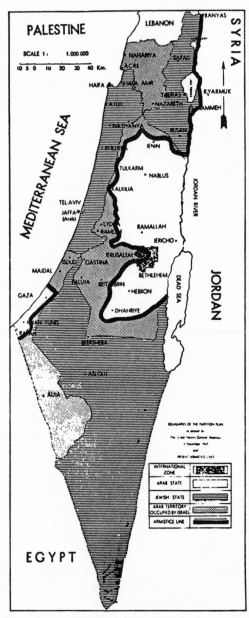

1949 Armistice lines.

salem, Nablus and Jenin, and the hill country around them, which is now called the "West Bank" of Jordan. It remained there after the armistice, and the late King Abdullah annexed this area and made it part of his kingdom, Jordan. But it was occupied by Israel in 1967, and 350,000 Arab inhabitants were driven east of the Jordan River, thus swelling the number of Palestinian refugees there.

In May 1950, to put an end to Arab talk of another round, the United States, Great Britain, and France issued a joint declaration stating that they would intervene if any attempt is made "to violate the frontiers or armistice lines."

To promote peace and stability in the area, this declaration was intended to serve notice to all concerned that it would not pay to attempt to change the armistice lines by force. For six years peace prevailed except for an occasional infiltration by a Palestinian into Israel, which always brought heavy reprisals against the adjoining Arab town or village by the Israeli military forces.

VII

Soviet Penetration Begins

In the beginning of their new life in refugee camps, the Palestinians were peaceful enough. They were confident that soon they would be repatriated, as war refugees usually are when hostilities cease. The United Nations had decreed, back in 1949, that Israel should permit them to return to their homes, so they daily expected to go back home. But as weeks and months, and even years, rolled by and no steps were taken to effect their return home, and as news of the flood of new Jewish immigrants into their country reached them, they became restive. Some individuals began to cross the long armistice line and plant a bomb here or a mine there. Israel retaliated massively against these "infiltrations."

The situation was aggravated early in 1955, when a group of refugees in the Gaza area, calling themselves *fedayeen*, began to cross the armistice line and harrass Israeli settlements in the Negeb. Israel answered with attacks on the Egyptian forces. The Egyptians, lacking modern weapons, suffered considerable losses.

President Nasser asked Washington and London to sell him arms to enable his army to defend itself. But both, bowing to Zionist objections, did not honor his request. Nor did they stop Israel's attacks. Then he turned to the East and was told that he could get weapons from Czechoslovakia and could pay for them with Egyptian cotton instead of hard cash.

This deal created a big stir in Washington and other Western capitals which feared Soviet penetration of the Middle East, hitherto a Western domain. Israel sounded the alarm and its leaders vowed to destroy these new arms before the Egyptians learned to use them. A good opportunity soon presented itself, and this threat was successfully carried out.

VIII

The Aswan Dam and the Suez War

To meet the needs of Egypt's rising population, Nasser decided to build the long-planned Aswan High Dam. Washington and London agreed to finance the preliminary works for the project. Some haggling about the terms of the loan followed. The U.S.S.R., too, offered financial aid, but the Egyptians preferred to deal with the West despite the West's denial of arms to them. On July 17, 1956, Egypt's ambassador to Washington returned from a visit to Cairo and announced that his government had decided to accept the loan on Washington's terms. But on July 19, Secretary of State John Foster Dulles told him that the offer had been withdrawn. Mr. Dulles thought that this humiliating rebuff would topple Nasser, who was evidently too independent to suit Dulles. Nasser had declined to join an alliance against Russia, preferring to remain uncommitted. Moreover, he had recently recognized China's Red government. But Moscow quickly came to Nasser's aid and provided the money and also the engineers to build the dam. When this dam was finally completed, it was U.S.S.R. President Nikolai Podgorny, not U. S. President Richard M. Nixon, who was the honored guest at the inauguration ceremonies in January 1971.

Nasser proved to be more durable than Mr. Dulles had

thought. He not only got the Aswan High Dam built without assistance from the West but he also struck back by nationalizing the Suez Canal Company, which operated the Suez Canal under a concession and was deriving a sizable profit from it. The British government was a part owner of this company; the rest of the stock was owned by French citizens. Prime Minister Anthony Eden did not like to lose the handsome income that his government was receiving in dividends on its shares. Moreover, he, like Dulles, resented Nasser's show of independence and considered his action a personal challenge to him. His ire was aroused.

Paris, too, disliked Nasser. His open support of the Algerian revolution was irritating to the Quai d'Orsay.

In addition, Nasser had closed the Gulf of 'Aqaba to Israeli shipping. Israel had established a settlement and had built a seaport at the extreme southern apex of Palestine, which touches on the northern end of the Gulf of 'Aqaba. This was named Elath. Egypt had blocked the one entrance to the gulf at its southern end which connects it with the Red Sea. Elath became useless as a seaport. But not for long. Ben-Gurion, who now was again Prime Minister after having retired from that post, had vowed in 1955 to open it "within twelve months." (This writer heard this on the radio while visiting Jerusalem.) He did.

Ben-Gurion, who had an abiding faith in force and never missed an opportunity to advance the cause of Zionism, quickly reached a secret agreement with London and Paris to attack Egypt jointly. But as late as October 25, Israel assured the U. N. Security Council that it would not start a war against its neighbors. And on October 28, Abba Eban told our department of state that Israel's mobilization was "purely defensive." Despite these pledges and despite President Eisenhower's public pleas against the use of force and the expression of his grave concern about war, the attack was launched on October 29, 1956. The Israeli army raced southward through Sinai toward the Suez Canal and Sharm

47

al-Sheikh. British and French forces landed at Port Said on the northern end of the Canal. The Egyptian army in Sinai was in peril, and Nasser's fate seemed doomed.

But Moscow again leaped to his rescue. Premier Bulganin sent messages to London, Paris, and Tel Aviv, demanding the immediate withdrawal of their forces and hinting at intervention if they failed to do so. He even rattled Russia's missiles in the process.

President Eisenhower strongly condemned the attack and asked the invaders to withdraw. Pursuant to his instructions, the United States delegation at the United Nations promptly introduced a resolution in the Assembly calling for immediate cease-fire and withdrawal of the foreign troops from Egyptian soil. So for the second time since the Second World War, Washington and Moscow found themselves working for the same end in a major case. The first time was when both voted for the partition of Palestine.

But when the Kremlin suggested that the United States join in military action to expel the invaders, President Dwight Eisenhower objected and alerted the United States armed forces for action against the Russians should they intervene. He felt that he was bound to do so under the North Atlantic Treaty, despite the fact that he held our allies guilty of unjustified aggression.

The American resolution was quickly approved by the United Nations General Assembly, and the combatants agreed to a cease-fire. London and Paris promptly began withdrawing their forces, and thus the third world war, which had seemed imminent, was averted.

Israel, although it had agreed to the cease-fire, refused to withdraw, ignoring three United Nations resolutions that called for withdrawl and rebuffing the personal pleadings of President Eisenhower. It wanted to stay on the banks of the Suez Canal and at Sharm al-Sheikh, Ben-Gurion said, to assure passage for its shipping through the Canal and through the Strait of Tiran, the one entrance to the Gulf of 'Aqaba, which was controlled from Sharm al-Sheikh.

After months of negotiations—some open, some secret—it was finally agreed that upon the withdrawal of the Israelis a United Nations force would be stationed at Sharm al-Sheikh to keep the strait of Tiran open and along the Israeli-Egyptian border to separate the troops and guard against Palestinian fedayeen activities. As the Israelis finally withdrew, United Nations troops were stationed at Sharm al-Sheikh and also along the Egyptian side of the border—Israel having refused to have any of them on its soil.

France and Britain did not achieve their war aims: the occupation of the Suez Canal and the banishment of President Nasser. Indeed, it was Prime Minister Anthony Eden who led his country into this war despite popular street demonstrations against it and despite the objections of some members of his cabinet, who became discredited, left his post, and permanently retired from politics. The only winner was Israeli Prime Minster Ben-Gurion. He succeeded in destroying the new Egyptian weapons and in opening the Gulf of 'Aqaba. So he alone was able to boast that his war aims had been achieved.

Egypt suffered heavy losses. Its new military equipment was destroyed by the enemy or simply abandoned by the troops when they were ordered to retreat to positions west of the Suez Canal. Egypt was also compelled to accept the stationing of United Nations troops at Sharm al-Sheikh to keep the strait of Tiran open. But Nasser remained at the helm and talked of the "victory" over the invaders.

Russia, which besides its vigorous pro-Egypt stand during the war, undertook immediately to reequip the Egyptian army and gained immensely in prestige among the Arabs. Its influence began to permeate every strata of Arab society. But President Eisenhower's stand in this war and his insistence on the withdrawal of the invaders from Egypt restored the faith of most Arabs in America's traditional fairness, and many thought that a new chapter, auguring continued improvement in Arab-American relations, had opened and eventually would triumph over Russia's influence.

IX

A Decade of Peace and Decline

Peace reigned in the Middle East for a whole decade following the 1956 invasion of Egypt by Israel, France, and Great Britain. The United Nations troops stationed at Sharm al-Sheikh and Gaza and along the border of Egypt with Israel at the end of that war did a good job of maintaining peace. They effectively prevented infiltration into Israel by the Palestinian fedayeen in Gaza and kept the Strait of Tiran open for Israeli shipping. Israel's southern border was now peaceful and secure, and Israeli settlements in the Negeb enjoyed complete freedom from fear. Along Israel's eastern frontier also there was peace and security for the Israelis during the decade that followed the 1956 war.

King Hussein's policy of moderation toward Israel and his uncompromising opposition to Communism are well known. And Jordan's limited resources made him financially and militarily dependent upon London and Washington, which made it necessary for him to follow their advice in foreign policy. So Jordan never was a menace to Israel. On the contrary, the Jordanian army's mission seems to have been limited to the maintenance of internal security. Amman never favored Palestinian commando activities against Israel. Hussein's ministers often explained that they opposed these actions because Israeli reprisals always caused heavier losses to Jordan. And they were right. Israel destroyed more than one Jordanian village in its reprisal attacks.

At any rate, Jordan's army, because of lack of modern weapons and an adequate air cover, never constituted a threat to Israel. King Hussein depended on Britain and the United States for protection against external aggression.

After a visit to Jordan's army headquarters and a tour of the Jordan-Israeli border in 1965 at the invitation of the then prime minister, the late Wasfi Tell, this writer was surprised to see this border devoid of any defenses and completely exposed. When this was mentioned to one of King Hussein's palace ministers, Mr. Jumaa, his reply was, "We don't need any defenses. Washington has assured us of the safety of our country."

But on June 8, 1967, after the Israeli occupation of the territory west of the Jordan River, King Hussein could only say, "Our friends have deserted us."

Hussein came to Washington later to plead for his country. He saw President Johnson and later President Nixon without success. But Washington rushed to his aid in 1970 when he was fighting the Palestinians.

Israel's northern border, too, was peaceful and secure. Lebanon did not even pretend to have a military force that could fight a foreign foe, certainly not Israel. Like Jordan, Lebanon depended upon the West for her security. Realizing her weakness, Lebanon did not participate in the 1967 war. But that has not spared her the repeated Israeli raids.

During a friendly chat with Lebanon's foreign minister in Beirut some years ago, this writer mentioned the absence of an adequate defense force for Lebanon. Grinning the foreign minister said: "What makes you think that? Don't you know that the Amir Mejid is our defense minister?" This prince, whom the writer had met briefly the previous day, was a well- and amply-built scion of an old family. He carried a revolver on his side at the time.

Like Jordan, to avoid Israeli reprisals, Lebanon had kept tight reins on the Palestinian refugees within her borders.

The situation on the Syrian border was different. Syrian leaders had always followed a hard and uncompromising line toward Israel. The Golan Heights, which they fortified, seems to have given them a false sense of security. Apparently they did not realize that in this age of jets, missiles, and napalm bombs, high ground no longer provides total security.

The Syrians talked toughly. They also attempted to prevent the Israelis from farming a demilitarized strip of land between them. Although they had been spending more than 50 percent of their annual budget on defense, their military preparations remained wholly inadequate. While some of Syria's temporary leaders more than once called for war against Israel, they themselves never built a fighting force that could cause Israel any concern.

Ahmed Shishekly, one of Syria's many presidents since 1948, in an address to the Arab Chambers of Commerce and Industry meeting in Damascus in 1953, assured his audience, "We will not sleep, we will not rest, until we liberate Palestine from Zionist rule." He was given a standing ovation for this brave statement. But a visit to his general staff headquarters two days later—he was chief of staff as well as president—left one wondering how and with what he was going to accomplish this liberation. Conversations with some officers and soldiers privately elsewhere did not change the poor impressions gained at the general staff headquarters.

Israel enjoyed a full decade of peace and security following the 1956 war. But this did not prove to be an unmixed blessing. The country did not thrive on it.

Although there was no shooting war and no threat of an immediate shooting war during the period 1957-1966, a state of war nevertheless existed between Israel and the Arab states. The 1948 Arab-Israeli war ended with an armistice, but no peace agreement was made. Likewise, the 1956 war ended with a cease-fire imposed by the United Nations. Again no peace agreement was concluded between Israel and Egypt. The state of war which came into being the day Israel was born has continued to this day. The Arabs have not recognized Israel as a state. But no Arab army has ever crossed its border—to be more accurate, the armistice line agreed upon in 1949. Not because the Arabs had become reconciled to Israel's existence in their midst but simply because they have never had a fighting force strong enough to challenge her.

Israel's armed forces have been at all times stronger than the combined forces of all the surrounding Arab states. This naturally acted as an effective deterrent. But to maintain such a powerful fighting force and keep it equipped with the latest weapons of war is costly, too costly for Israel's economic capacity. Were it not for the generous economic aid of the United States Government, Israel would not have been able to maintain such a force, despite the heavy taxes saddled upon its people, the compulsory loans imposed on Israeli workers, the so-called indemnity collected from West Germany, and the generosity of American Jews who have poured billions into the economy of the Jewish state.

Some of the Arab states tried to arm, but their financial resources were limited. Sources of arms, too, were limited. Moreover, the Arab peoples lagged behind the Israelis in technology. So their efforts were utterly inadequate despite their numerical superiority. But the talk of "preparation for the next round" made the leaders popular with the masses. It also helped Israel obtain more money from the United States.

The state of Israel was to be destroyed and the Israelis were to be thrown into the sea. In the early '50s, this writer met one of the Arab ambassadors in New York, who proudly showed him the draft of a speech he planned to deliver at the U. N. General Assembly. It was an excellent speech for delivery in Cairo or Damascus or, better still, in a refugee camp in Jordan. But not in the General Assembly in New York. I suggested that he tone it down a little and reminded him of Theodore Roosevelt's famous advice, "Speak softly but carry a big stick." His excellency thought for a moment and then sadly said, "But I don't have a big stick."

However, there was one weapon available to the Arabs that cost them little and that they used effectively. This was the boycott, which world Jewry had used against Hitler's Germany and others and which the United States used in both world wars under the Trading with the Enemy Act.

Since a state of war continued to exist between the Arabs and Israel, trade between them was obviously prohibited. Israel could not trade with her neighbors. Nor could an Israeli citizen cross its land border in any direction, a fact that caused Moshe Dayan's son, Udi, to say to this writer that he "would love to be able to drive to Beirut," which he had been told is a beautiful city. Israelis desiring to leave or enter the country could do so by sea or by air over the Mediterranean Sea.

The Arabs extended this boycott to foreign individuals and corporations who did certain types of business with Israel. A tourist with an Israeli visa on his passport could not enter an Arab country.

This boycott, which is still in force although punctured here and there by resourceful Jews or avaricious Arabs, nevertheless hurt Israel's economy and contributed to make the country a veritable ghetto.

The years that followed the 1949 armistice witnessed a rush of Jewish immigrants to Israel, which soon tripled its 1948 Jewish population of 650,000. But the sources of immigration seemed to dry up in the early '60s. In some years, the number of those who came to settle in the Promised Land were barely equal to the number of those who left it.[10] Jews living in Western Europe and the Americas, enjoying equal rights with their countrymen and prosperous, have shown little desire to

10. The number of Jews who left Israel during the period 1948 to 1969 exceeded 200,000, according to the *Israel Year Book for 1960*.

exchange a life of freedom and affluence for a life of austerity in beseiged Israel.

Although peace continued to reign immigration lagged. It dropped from 52,000 in 1964 to 30,000 in 1965 and to 14,000 in 1966. More than 35,000, mostly professionals or skilled technicians, left Israel in 1966. Many American Jews began to feel that Israel should now stand on its own feet economically. They had contributed to its support generously during its formative period and even more generously during her two wars. Now that it was strong and enjoying peace and security, they felt that it should be self-supporting. The immigrants, for whose resettlement they had opened their pocketbooks, were now few. The Arabs were not a menace. There was no good reason they should continue to send their earnings to Israel. So their cash contributions decreased or completely stopped. Official Washington felt the same way and planned to phase out outright grants from the United States Treasury.

In the meantime, Israel's imports continued to exceed its exports, and the decline of the Israeli pound was accelerated.[11] Israel's industrial production dropped 11 percent in 1966. The general economy suffered and unemployment exceeded 10 percent, presenting a serious problem. The unemployed began to demonstrate in the streets.

Time magazine, in its issue of April 7, 1967, reported that corporate profits had fallen 15 percent, that unemployment had risen to 10 percent of the working force, that thousands were on the dole, and that 7,000 jobless persons had marched through Tel Aviv demanding "bread and work." More significant, 12,000 Israelis had recently emigrated from Israel.

In vain did Prime Minister Eshkol try to reassure the people. Because he himself was frightened, he was not convincing.

---

11. In 1972 the rate dropped to four Israeli pounds to the dollar. In November 1974, it was devalued to six pounds to the dollar. It is now eighteen pounds to the dollar.

Israel was sick and in need of strong medicine—something like war. And the time for it was most favorable.

X

To War, To War

As various measures taken to cure the depression proved ineffective and the future grew darker, the government of Israel decided on the one sure remedy: war.

A victorious campaign against the Arabs (while they were so weak and divided) could bring great rewards. It also might force the Arabs to end the twenty-year-old state of war, sign a peace treaty, end the boycott, and open Arab markets to Israeli economic penetration, thus enabling the state to become self-supporting and viable. It could also permit the acquisition of additional territory for strategic purposes and to accommodate more Jewish immigrants. The temptation was obviously strong. Moreover, victory, by every reckoning, seemed certain. The possibility of defeat was practically nil. And what if defeat should come? Isn't the American Sixth Fleet cruising nearby, watching and listening, its jets, its long-range guns, and its marines ready to spring into action if the need should arise? War in this instance offered great rewards and little or no risk. So Tel Aviv began to prepare for war and also to look for an excuse.

The time was most propitious. The Egyptians were fighting the royalists in Yemen, who were being supported by Saudi Arabia. Egypt and Syria were making faces at King Hussein

57

of Jordan. The latter, fearing an attack, had sent the bulk of Jordan's army to the Syrian border, which caused Damascus to charge on May 15, 1967, that Jordan and Israel were planning a joint attack on Syria. Jordan then expelled the Syrian ambassador to Amman. The Palestinian leadership was busy plotting to topple King Hussein. Iraq was torn by a civil war. Nasser was disliked by President Johnson who had stopped the sale of wheat to Egypt to embarrass him. And Syria had just had another coup. The time, indeed, was most favorable.

Israel's very efficient intelligence organization had all the information needed. General Herzog, the commander of Israel's air force, posing as a German, went to Cairo, ingratiated himself with the top brass, and obtained their deepest secrets in detail. And, of course, Israel had access to all the information gathered by all the United States agencies, including the C.I.A.

Palestinian guerillas had begun to escalate their activities in the late summer of 1966, thus giving Israel an excuse for war. In November 1966, Israel, asserting that Palestinian guerillas or "terrorists" were operating from the Jordanian town of Samou, mounted a massive attack against it. According to U.N. count, 152 persons were killed or wounded and 127 buildings were destroyed. But this attack did not develop into war. Jordan judiciously did not accept the challenge. Amman contented itself with complaining to the United Nations Security Council which found the attack unjustified and condemned Israel.

Since King Hussein was then unpopular with his Arab neighbors, Cairo's Voice of the Arabs attacked him for his "failure to protect his people." Amman promptly taunted Nasser for opening the Gulf of 'Aqaba to Israeli shipping and chided him for pretending to be brave while protected by United Nations troops. Nasser was deeply stung. It was his desire to remove this sting which caused Nasser, some six months later, to order the withdrawal of the United Nations' troops from Egypt and announce the closing of 'Aqaba to

Israeli shipping, thus giving Israel an excuse for starting the war against him.

Jordan increased its patrol units along its border with Israel to prevent the fedayeen from crossing into Israel. Many of them then moved to Syria and began to harass Israel on her northeastern border.

Israel threatened Syria if it did not curb the commandos. A Syrian spokesman replied that his country was not obligated "to protect Israel from her victims. We are not willing," he said, "to become the protectors of the Arabs' enemy with whom we are at war."

Syria thus gave Israel another excuse to strike, and strike she did on April 7, 1967. Syria's losses in this attack included five war jets.

But again a general war did not follow the attack. Syria, which for years had been calling on the Arabs to renew the war against Israel, followed Jordan's example and contented herself with complaining to the United Nations.

On April 11, four days after the attack on Syria, Israel's Prime Minister Eshkol said that the United States Sixth Fleet in the Mediterranean would come to Israel's aid when needed. Could the Arabs challenge the might of the United States?

Israel was again disappointed but continued to move toward war.

Months before the war started, Jewish youths from the United States and other countries began to pour into Tel Aviv's Lod Airport to join Israel's armed forces or to man her factories. Many of the young men who came to fight for Israel already had military training in their native countries, some with the regular forces of the country, some in special Jewish training camps.

The fact that they were citizens of other countries was ignored by them and by the governments of their native lands. Our Department of State was embarrassed when the legality of American citizens fighting for a foreign country was raised. Its comment was that "they were not many."

Money, too, began to pour in as soon as the Jews in the

diaspora were told that war was coming. A Zionist fund raiser, Gottlieb Hammer, told Lawrence Mosher of the *National Observer* later, "When the blood flows the money flows."[12] The contributions were generous—hundreds of millions of dollars a year since 1967. Zionist leaders had organized the Israel Defense Fund in the United States and obtained income-tax exemption on contributions to it despite the fact that it was a foreign nation's war chest and not "religious," "charitable," or "educational" to qualify it for such exemption. So contributions to this fund, like those to the United Jewish Appeal, which also collected money for Israel, were easy to make.[13] And the sale of Israeli bonds in the United States boomed.

In addition, the Zionists in the United States and Europe inauguarated a propaganda campaign that pictured Israel as a peaceful little lamb which was about to be attacked by a pack of hungry Arab wolves. This campaign, aided by boastings and empty threats by some Arabs, was very effective.

On May 11, 1967, Prime Minister Levi Eshkol made a statement in which he referred to Palestinian sabotage activities and threatened "to adopt measures no less drastic than those of April 7" unless these activities stop. A similar warning was sent to the United Nations Security Council. As he spoke, Israel was already mobilizing and Israeli troops were moving toward the Syrian border.

About ten days after issuing his warning, Prime Minister Eshkol told the Knesset that Israel was willing to withdraw the troops sent to the Egyptian border if Egypt would recall forty or fifty thousand sent into Sinai. Cairo apparently did not hear this belated proffer of the olive branch and did not

---

12. *National Observer,* May 18, 1970.

13. On March 14, 1968, the American Council on the Middle East, an organization of Americans interested in a lasting peace in the Holy Land, wrote the secretary of the treasury questioning the legality of the exemption but was given the brush-off. President Nixon did not wish to lift it.

respond to it. Or did Nasser ignore it because he recalled a similar speech by Ben-Gruion just before the Israeli forces attacked in 1956?

Alarmed by the troop movements, Syria alerted her ally, Cairo, and some of the foreign ambassadors in Damascus. Syria's chargé d'affaires in Washington met with U.S. Assistant Secretary of State Lucius D. Battle and told him that Israel was about to attack Syria.

Tel Aviv's foreign ministry replied that what the Syrians called "troops" were tourists out seeing the sights.

In the meantime, Prime Minister Eshkol, while threatening the Arabs, told his people that the very existence of their state was being threatened. He told the Knesset that "Israel's life hung by a thread." But shortly thereafter General Haim Herzog, who ought to know better, apparently to allay any fear that may have been aroused by the prime minister's statements, told the Israelis, "Knowing the facts, I can say that if I had a choice between sitting in an Egyptian aircraft sent to bomb Tel Aviv and sitting in a house in Tel Aviv, then I would prefer for the good of my health to sit in Tel Aviv."

In a newspaper discussion concerning the real causes of the war, General Matetiyahu Peled said in March 1972, "All those stories about the huge danger we were facing because of our small territorial size . . . had never been considered in our calculations prior to unleashing of hostilities."

General Peled also said that this was nothing but a bluff that was born and bred after the war.

In its issue of April 4, 1972, the news paper *Ma'ariv* quoted General Ezer Weizman, chief of operations during the war, as saying, "There never was a danger of extermination. This hypothesis had never been considered in any serious meeting."

On April 19, 1972, *Ma'ariv* reported that the former chief of staff General Haim Bar-Lev, had stated, "We were not threatened with genocide on the eve of the Six Day War and we had never thought of such a possibility."

Obviously Israel's military leaders, who knew the innermost

secrets of the enemy, were never aware of the danger that Prime Minister Eshkol feared so much, and they never discussed it.

True, Palestinian leader Ahmed Shukeiry, who since has been rejected by his people, did make some terrible threats against Israel, but no one took his threats seriously. Certainly Israeli leaders did not. It is also true that after both sides had mobilized, President Nasser made some strong threats "if war comes." But he also pledged not to fire the first shot.

Eshkol was correct in saying that Israel's existence was then in danger. But this danger did not come from the Arabs, as he wished the world to believe. The danger came from within. It was inherent in the very nature of the state. This danger, averted by Israel's victory in the Six Day war, has not been permanently eliminated. It is still there and is raising its head once again.

Syria had a mutual defense treaty with Egypt signed in November 1966 in hope of deterrring Israel. So Damascus notified Cairo of the grave situation on its border. President Nasser ordered Egyptian troops and tanks to cross the Suez Canal into Sinai, where they soon were massacred by Israeli napalm bombs. On May 21, 1967, total mobilization was ordered by Egypt.

On May 30, King Hussein made a dramatic flight to Cairo and signed a defense treaty with Nasser, his old enemy. On June 4, Iraq also joined the alliance. "The noose was being tightened around Israel's neck," lamented the pro-Israel American press. Sympathy for Israel soared.

President Nasser declared that he did not want war and would not fire the first shot. Evidently he was sincere in making this statement, for he knew the weakness of his forces. He had learned this in the Yemen war into which he had plunged Egypt years before and which was still going on, its end not yet in sight. He knew that his country was already weary of war and that it would be suicidal to start a new war before finishing the old one. Moreover, President Johnson had quietly warned him against starting a war. He later explained that the order to call up the reserves and to send troops toward the border was issued in hope of deterring Israel.

According to the *Washington Observer Newsletter* of July 15, 1967, President Johnson also assured Israeli Prime Minister Eshkol that he would send American forces to aid Israel if the battle turned against her, and Johnson actually alerted two airborne divisions for action if necessary.

Nasser did not know that Israel was not to be so easily deterred. Nor did he know that Israel was mobilizing against Egypt, not against Syria. Israeli leaders wanted to seize the opportunity presented by Arab dissention and weakness to end all Arab resistance and force the Arabs to recognize Israel and sign a peace treaty with her, and thus end the state of war and the boycott. This was Israel's demand after the war, in addition to new "secure" borders. They knew, of course, that the main strength of the Arabs was on the Nile, not on the Jordan. But Egypt hitherto had given Israel no cause for war. So they directed their threats against Syria, knowing that Egypt was bound under the alliance mentioned above to come to Syria's aid. They used the activities of the Palestinians as an excuse.

Nasser unwittingly soon provided an excuse for war against him. He first ordered mobilization "to defend Syria if attacked." This, of course, not only was his prerogative but also his duty under the mutual defense treaty with Syria. On May 16, Cairo asked for the withdrawal of the United Nations' peace-keeping force stationed at Sharm al-Sheikh deep inside Egypt and along Egypt's border with Israel "for their safety" in case of war.[14] This, too, could not be regarded as a *casus belli*, especially since he had stated that he would not fire the first shot. And he did not.

United Nations Secretary General U Thant, who had gone

---

14. Despite this precaution, eleven members of the U.N. force in Gaza were killed by the rapidly advancing Israelis—unintentionally, of course.

to the area on May 22, hoping to prevent the outbreak of hostilities, found himself obligated to comply with Egypt's request. He realized that the United Nations could not station troops in any country without that country's consent. He realized also that the presence of these troops along the border would have a quieting influence on the explosive situation. So he asked Israel to allow them on her side of the border. Israel refused, categorically,[15] as it did back in 1956 when the U.N. tried to place its peace-keeping troops on both sides of the border. So the secretary general had no alternative but to withdraw them when Egypt asked him to do so. Indeed, Israel even refused to let them withdraw across her border in order to avoid being caught in the cross fire.

---

15. At the end of the 1948 war, the United Nations established a mixed commission to patrol the armistice lines and maintain peace. But Israel had denounced the commission operating on its borders with Egypt and boycotted its meetings several years before.

XI

The Drums of War Beat Louder

President Nasser, who had on previous occasions rejected war with Israel on the ground that the Arabs were not ready for it while half of Egypt's army was still bogged down in Yemen and unable to subdue the royalist forces, now gave Israel a more plausible excuse for war than the Palestinians.

Nasser's prestige, which had reached a very low level because of his inability to win or end the war in Yemen, began to rise. He seemed to be master of the situation and spoke confidently. But although his generals assured him that they could win in a war with Israel, he still did not want war.

Having safely removed the United Nations troops from his country, the president of Egypt decided to go a step further and wipe out the last stigma from his record with Israel. On May 22, 1967, he declared, that the Strait of Tiran would henceforth be closed to Israeli shipping. This action sent his prestige among the Arabs rocketing.

But Cairo miscalculated sadly. Israel's leaders had already decided on war, and Tel Aviv's hand was on the trigger, ready to pull it. The blockade, which was a nominal one, offered a better excuse than the actions of the Palestinian fedayeen.

So Israeli leaders now forgot Syria and the Palestinians and began to harp on Tiran. Nasser was "choking Israel," they complained.

According to the United States Department of Commerce, no Israeli flagship had passed through Tiran during the preceding two years while the strait was under the control of United Nations troops and open to Israeli shipping, and only 2 percent of Israel's foreign trade had passed through while Tiran was open. The Israel Ship Line sails from Mediterranean ports. During the crisis, the Israelis arranged to charter a ship and sail her through Tiran and thus create an "incident" if Egypt attempted to turn her back. But they had difficulties hiring enough sailors to man her. Then they realized that the delay would alert Cairo and give her time to prepare, which would ruin their plan to make a surprise attack. So they abandoned the plan and thus dulled Cairo into the belief that confrontation was not contemplated. (See the *Washington Post,* July 1, 1967.) The United Nations Security Council, which was already grappling with the crisis in continuous sessions, might find a solution to the problem before the ship was ready.

Like many Arab actions intended for intra-Arab purposes only, Nasser's blockade boomeranged outside the Arab world and he began to beat a retreat. He soon realized that his announcement of the blockade was hasty and unwise. So he offered to have the matter submitted to the International Court of Justice, pledging to abide by that court's decision should it uphold Israel's claimed right to free navigation through the strait.

A decision by the International Court of Jutice in favor of Israel, or the Washington proposal of a joint declaration, would have permitted Nasser to rescind the blockade without losing face. He seemed to have been anxious to extricate himself from this hasty move, and to that end he arranged for his vice-president, Zakaria Muhieddin, to go to Washington in an attempt to reach a solution. This was announced in Cairo on June 3. Muhieddin was to see the president on June 7. (The war broke out on June 5, and Muhieddin's trip had to be cancelled.)

Patrick Sealy of the *Washington Post* cabled from Cairo on

May 25 in part: "There is a certain nervousness but no real feeling that war is near. No public excitement. No rush to banks or hoarding. For a vast majority of Egyptians life continues as before."

The prime minister of Israel announced on May 28 that his government had decided to rely on "the continuation of political action in the world arena" to open Tiran.

To avoid "incidents," Egypt, on May 31, asked the U.N. to reactivate the Mixed Armistice Commission, which had supervised the border but had been stopped by Israel years earlier.

On Saturday evening, June 3, in an interview with British Conservative Minister Anthony Nutting, Nasser said, "The Middle East situation had eased" and indicated that the Russians felt that "war should be avoided."

Egypt and the world breathed easier. The talks in Washington, considering Nasser's now moderate attitude, were very likely to result in a solution.

So Egypt's air force officers in the Cairo area decided to hold the song-and-dance party that had been planned some time back but had been postponed because of the tense situation. They did hold it on the evening of June 4. But when they awoke the next morning, they found that their aircraft had been destroyed and the war was nearly over.

In reality, however, Israel feared these moves meant a solution. She was not interested in merely keeping Tiran open to her shipping. She wanted Tiran and Sharm al-Sheikh to have and to hold permanently.

The strait in question lies between a point on the southernmost corner of the Sinai peninsula called Sharm al-Sheikh and a small Egyptian island called Tiran. The occupation of this area would enable Israel to control navigation not only in the Gulf of 'Aqaba but also in the Gulf of Suez, which connects the Suez Canal with the Red Sea. It would place Jordan's entire maritime trade at her mercy, for Jordan has only one seaport, 'Aqaba, on the northern end of the Gulf. It would also control all traffic through the Suez Canal.

That is why Sharm al-Sheikh was a primary target of the

Israel's 1967 conquests.

68

war, and that is why Israelis say they will not give it up.

When Tel Aviv heard of Muhiedden's forthcoming visit to Washington, it feared a solution, even one opening the Strait of Tiran, and decided to act fast. Her war cabinet, which now included Gen. Moshe Dayan—the hero of the 1956 war—as defense minister, held a very important session on June 4, which was attended by Israel's ambassador to Washington. Having already decided on war, mobilized for it, and called in Dayan to conduct it, the cabinet now decided to strike at once. But to lull the Arabs further, they made no mention of war, although they voted to increase the income tax by an addition-al 10 percent to meet its expenses. Here is the cabinet's announced action at this meeting as reported by the *Jerusalem Post* the following morning: "The Cabinet yesterday voiced concern over the slowness with which the Powers are acting to lift the blockade of the Tiran straits, and decided on the lines along which diplomatic action will be intensified in the capitals of the maritime powers."

"Diplomatic action," indeed!

As the world now knows, Israel struck early on June 5, 1967, before this newspaper was out on the streets, and within three hours destroyed some four hundred Arab war planes, mostly on the ground, and the war for all practical purposes was over. Ground forces are sitting ducks for the party that controls the air. Israel now did. The little lamb that was bleating in fear of being gobbled up by the wolves was now itself gobbling up the so-called wolves.

The Israelis ignored the United Nations' calls for cease-fire until they had reached all their predetermined goals—the Suez Canal and Sharm al-Sheikh in Egypt, the Jordan River in Jordan, and lastly the city of al-Kuneitra in the Golan District of Syria. In order to give the Israelis more time to complete the conquest of the Golan region, United States Ambassador Arthur J. Goldberg absented himself from the United Nations and thus managed to delay another call for cease-fire.

The *Jewish Press*, in its issue of September 15, 1967, let the cat out of the bag, saying that Zionist Goldberg "took a long walk" in order "to buy time for Israel to gain as much Syrian territory as possible before any cease-fire went into effect." The disappearance of Goldberg delayed action by the Security Council for six hours on a third resolution calling for cease-fire on the Syrian front. So Goldberg played Joshua who stopped the sun to enable the Israelites to finish off the defeated Amorites at Gibeon. (Josh. 10:12-13.)

While three columns of Israeli troops and tanks were racing toward the Suez Canal and Sharm al-Sheikh, Prime Minister Eshkol took to the air and told his people, "Since the early hours today our armed forces on land and in the air have been repulsing the attack of the aggressive Egyptian forces."

Mr. Eshkol's ambassador to the United Nations, Gideon Rafael, awakened United Nations Security Council President Hans Tabor of Denmark at 3:10 A.M. (New York time) to tell him, "I have just received reports that Egyptian land and air forces have moved against Israel and Israeli forces are now engaged in repelling them."

Minutes later, Ambassador M. Awad El Kony of Egypt told Tabor that Israel had launched "a treacherous, pre-meditated" attack against his country.

Before the day was over, Eshkol jubilantly declared, "The enemy is nowhere in sight and our land forces are proceeding as scheduled."[16]

The prime minister thus tacitly admitted that Egypt did not start the war. How could the Egyptians have started the war if they were "nowhere in sight" right at the beginning?

When it became obvious that the war was started by Israel, Tel Aviv said that its action was "preemptive." But, as we have seen, Israel's military leaders have stated that Israel was never in danger. The fact that the Egyptian forces were on the run from the very beginning corroborates their judgment.

---

16. *Washington Post*, June 6, 1973, p. A15.

Three days before the war started, Ygal Allon, then deputy prime minister and later foreign minister said, "There is not the slightest doubt about the outcome of this war, and each of its stages, and we are not forgetting the Jordanian and Syrian fronts either."

Note that he talked of "this war" as if it already had started. Allon knew that the cabinet had already decided on war. He and his colleagues also knew that the Arabs were not ready for war and didn't want war. General Rabin, who now heads the Israeli cabinet, has said: "I do not believe that Nasser wanted war. The two divisions he sent into Sinai on May 14 would not have been enough to unleash an all-out war."

Obviously it was Israel, not the Arabs, that wanted war. The campaign was so well planned and so brilliantly executed that Israeli losses in it were under seven hundred men. Arab losses in both men and materiel were staggering.

King Hussein of Jordan, his troops on the run with the Israelis already on the banks of the Jordan River in hot pursuit, welcomed the first United Nations call for cease-fire. Egypt and Syria quickly followed suit. Israel procrastinated until its troops reached their predetermined objectives. In six days, during all of which they were constantly on the offensive, they occupied the Gaza strip and Jordan's West Bank, thus completing the occupation of all of Palestine, all Egyptian territory east of the Suez Canal and the Gulf of Suez, and Syria's Golan district, including the strategic town of Al-Kuneitra.

As had been expected, Israel was truly rejuvenated. Her economy, supported by generous, tax-exempt contributions from American Jews, the sale of Israel bonds in the United States, and United States loans and grants as well as Jewish tourists who flocked to see the results of her amazing victory, simply boomed. Faith in the state's viability was restored. Immigration was accelerated. And a global campaign to compel the U.S.S.R. to permit larger numbers of Jews to emigrate to Israel was inaugurated. The United States provided the money for settling the newcomers. In 1972 the United States Government gave Israel a gift of $85,000,000 to build homes for the newly arriving Soviet Jews. This was followed by another gift of $50,000,000. A building boom was thus created in Israel.

But though Israel did win a brilliant victory in 1967, she did not win peace with the Arabs. She preferred their territory to peace. She remained at war, surrounded by enemies, and dependent on America and American Jewry for survival. America has been more than willing to open her treasury and her arsenal to Israel and provide her both cash and arms for the asking. So there was no need to evacuate the newly conquered territories, especially Jerusalem, Sharm Al-Sheikh, and the Egyptian oil fields in Abu Rudeis, in order to win peace.

XII

The Expansionist Plans Unveiled

When Arab Jerusalem fell on June 7, Foreign Minister Eban declared, "We have returned to Jerusalem never to part from her again." General Dayan made a similar statement. A few days later Israel annexed the city. Arab homes adjacent to the Moslem holy shrine of Al Haram, which contains the Dome of the Rock, were leveled to provide space for Jewish worshipers in front of the "Wailing Wall," a part of Al Haram but regarded as a remnant of the vanished Jewish Temple. Other Arab lands in and around Jerusalem were expropriated for the purpose of erecting new housing facilities for new Jewish immigrants, thus diluting the Arab population of the Holy City as part of the process of Judaising it.

As Israeli troops advanced eastward through Jordan's West Bank, Arab civilians were "encouraged" to leave their homes and seek safety east of the river. Palestinian refugees in camps in the Jordan Valley were sent across the river. The process of emptying the occupied land of its Arab population continued long after the guns were silenced until Amman and the International Red Cross finally succeeded in stemming the tide. But not before the government of Jordan was saddled with the problem of caring for 350,000 new refugees, some of them refugees for the second time.

Jewish settlements were also established at Hebron, along the west bank of the Jordan River, and in the Golan district of Syria. Hotels and houses were built at Sharm al-Sheikh, which Israeli spokesmen have said should remain in Israeli hands. A road connecting Sharm al-Sheikh with Elath was cut along the western shore of the Gulf of 'Aqaba at considerable cost.

Since the 1967 war, Israel has been pumping oil from wells drilled by the Egyptians at Abu Rudeis in Sinai. These wells have been supplying Israel with a considerable part of her oil needs—over two hundred million dollars worth each year.

The Suez Canal, the great artery of commerce between East and West, and particularly between the Persian Gulf and the Mediterranean, was closed to traffic by the war. The closing of this canal deprived Egypt of more than two hundred million dollars a year in income and caused Western Europe, Japan, and the United States to spend billions of dollars in extra shipping costs, especially for Arab and Iranian oil. The tankers carrying this oil have had to go around Africa in order to reach their destinations, thus traveling more than twice the distance.

At the risk of sounding like "I told you so," we wish to call attention to the fact that all this was predicted by this author when the partition resolution was adopted by the U.N. General Assembly. In my book *Palestine Dilemma,* published early in 1948, it was stated on page 218 that the Zionists, who then pushed for the partition resolution and celebrated wildly when it was adopted, would not be satisfied with it. We predicted that they would eventually endeavor to take Jerusalem and that they would also "demand the annexation of this or that part of Arab territory, if only for the purpose of 'rectifying' their curvilinear frontiers."

Before the manuscript was published in 1948, they took part of Jerusalem and half of the territory reserved for the Arab state, thus improving greatly upon the boundaries drawn by the U.N. As the result of the 1967 war, they took and promptly annexed the rest of Jerusalem and began to demand "secure boundaries." Just where these boundaries should be they have not yet said. But everyone knows that today, with faster and faster war planes and deadlier intercontinental missiles, there are no secure boundaries anywhere on earth.

XIII

Peace: How To Prevent It

When Nasser announced the closing of the Strait of Tiran, President Johnson promptly branded the action as illegal. Johnson also warned Nasser not to start a war or he would "suffer the consequences." United States Ambassador to Cairo Richard H. Nolte told Egyptian Foreign Minister Mahmoud Riad that President Johnson wanted Egypt to guarantee freedom of shipping for Israel through the Gulf of 'Aqaba before sending Egyptian troops to Sharm al-Sheikh. This was rejected by Riad, who also told the ambassador that Egypt would consider the United States Israel's partner if Israel attacked any Arab country.

On May 23, 1967, the president issued the following warning:

> To the leaders of all the nations of the Near East, I wish to say what three American presidents have said before me—that the United States is firmly committed to the support of the political independence and territorial integrity of all the nations of that area. The United States strongly opposes aggression by anyone in the area, in any form, overt or clandestine. This has been the policy of the United States led by four presidents—President

Truman, President Eisenhower, President Kennedy, and myself—as well as the policy of both our political parties.

On May 26, Israeli Foreign Minister Abba Eban conferred with United States Secretary of Defense Robert S. McNamara and President Johnson. What transpired at these conferences has not yet been published.

Later that day, Robert H. Estabrook of the *Washington Post* reported from the United Nations that the United States had "extensive commitments" to defend Israel's rights of navigation in the Gulf of 'Aqaba" which "have astonished even high State Department officials" when they saw them. Estabrook cited "an Israeli source" for his report.

With such clear warning from the most powerful nation on earth, is it any wonder that Nasser had second thoughts about the closing of 'Aqaba to Israeli flagships? As previously stated, Nasser had pledged publicly not to fire the first shot and secretly hoped that Israel, too, would not do so. But his hopes were soon dashed to the ground.

The Israeli victory in the Six Day War changed President Johnson's views concerning the "territorial integrity of all the nations of the area." He opposed United Nations resolutions calling for Israeli withdrawal from the Arab territories occupied during the fighting, and he echoed Israel's demands for "secure borders," *de jure* recognition of, and peace agreements with Israel. This formula was presented to the Security Council by Ambassador Arthur Goldberg.

To his credit, however, President Johnson did not approve of Israel's ambitious plans of expansion. *Newsweek* magazine of January 22, 1968, reported that he had told Israeli Prime Minister Eshkol: "You are asking me to guarantee your borders. What borders do you want me to guarantee?"

What the president wanted to achieve was to throw Nasser out and force the Arabs to cede some territory to straighten out Israel's frontiers, recognize her, and enter into a peace treaty with her.

As the bitter debate continued at the United Nations, the United States gave Israel eighty Skyhawk jets and other military equipment "to replace her losses" in the war and to deter the Arabs from attempting to regain their occupied lands. Johnson also authorized the transfer to Israel of fifty F4 Phantom jets, to compensate her for fifty French war planes Israel had contracted to buy and which President DeGaulle embargoed because he held that Israel was the aggressor in the war. DeGaulle also embargoed the shipment of arms to all Middle East countries as a step to prevent a new war.

America had its own casualties in this war. The *Liberty*, a spy ship, while in international waters 15 miles north of the coast of Sinai (monitoring the fighting there) was continuously attacked by Israeli jets and torpedo boats for 26 minutes. Thirty-four Americans were killed and one hundred and sixty-four wounded. Israel said that the ship, which was flying the American flag, was mistaken for an Egyptian vessel. Talks of investigating the incident were hushed up.

While the United States vigorously backed Israel's demands at the United Nations, the U.S.S.R. delegation, led by Premier Kosygin, espoused the Arab cause. The debate dragged on and on.

In an effort to break this impasse, Premier Kosygin and President Johnson met privately at Glassboro, New Jersey, on June 23 and again on June 25, 1967. But the two days of discussion produced no agreement. The meeting, however, announced to the world that settlement of the Arab-Israeli impasse depended more on the two superpowers than on the antagonists themselves.

In late September, Secretary of State Dean Rusk met with Israeli Foreign Minister Eban in Washington and then announced that America's policy was one of "inaction" until the Arabs "are willing to consider a settlement." Israel now was demanding a "peace pact" before discussing a settlement.

Finally the British delegate to the United Nations submitted a draft resolution that both sides, now tired and weary, thought was acceptable. As adopted on November 22, 1967, Resolution 242 stated:

The Security Council,

Expressing its continuing concern with the grave situation in the Middle East,

Emphasizing the inadmissibility of the acquisition of territory by war and the need to work for a just and lasting peace in which every State in the area can live in security,

Emphasizing further that all Member States in their acceptance of the Charter of the United Nations have undertaken a commitment to act in accordance with Article 2 of the Charter,

1. *Affirms* that the fulfilment of Charter principles requires the establishment of a just and lasting peace in the Middle East which should include the application of both the following principles:

  (i) Withdrawal of Israeli armed forces from territories occupied in the recent conflict;

  (ii) Termination of all claims or states of belligerency and respect for and acknowledgement of the sovereignty, territorial integrity and political independence of every State in the area and their right to live in peace within secure and recognized boundaries free from threats or acts of force;

2. *Affirms further* the necessity

  (a) For guaranteeing freedom of navigation through international waterways in the area;

  (b) For achieving a just settlement of the refugee problem;

  (c) For guaranteeing the territorial inviolability and political independence of every State in the area, through measures including the establishment of demilitarized zones;

3. *Requests* the Secretary-General to designate a Special Representative to proceed to the Middle East to

establish and maintain contacts with the States concerned in order to promote agreement and assist efforts to achieve a peaceful and accepted settlement in accordance with the provisions and principles in this resolution;

4. *Requests* the Secretary-General to report to the Security Council on the progress of the efforts of the Special Representative as soon as possible.

United Nations Secretary-General U Thant promptly appointed Swedish Ambassador to Moscow Dr. Gunnar V. Jarring as his representative for the purpose of implementing this resolution. Ambassador Jarring established headquarters at Cyprus and soon became a regular commuter between Tel Aviv, Cairo, and Amman. He did not go to Damascus because Syria had rejected the resolution as unfair to the Arabs. The Palestinians, too, thought it was unfair and declared their opposition to it.

Ambassador Jarring's visits to the Arab capitals and to Israel produced no results. Likewise, his conferences in New York with the ambassadors of the governments concerned produced no progress.

Soon after his election to the presidency in November 1968, Richard M. Nixon dispatched William W. Scranton, former governor of Pennsylvania, to the Middle East to study the situation and recommend to him what United States policy should be. Scranton, after visiting the area, recommended an "even-handed" policy. This aroused the ire of the Zionists and perhaps also of Dr. Henry Kissinger, President Nixon's foreign policy adviser, who later told newsmen that the White House policy (of which he was the architect) was designed "to eject the U.S.S.R. from the Middle East." Of course, Russia geographically is partly in the Middle East. It borders on Turkey and Iran, both important Middle East countries, and both adjoining Arab territories. Perhaps he meant that by continuing to support Israel, the Russians would pull out of

Egypt. If so, he ignored the fact that it was America's blind support of Israel that helped the Soviet Union to establish its presence on the Nile.

In the spring of 1969, President Nasser of Egypt, despairing of peace through United Nations' special representative Jarring, decided that he would not allow the 1967 cease-fire line to become a permanent border as the 1949 armistice line in Palestine, by inaction, had become Israel's permanent border. He started "a war of attrition," and Egyptian guns on the west side of the Suez Canal began to fire at the Israelis, now deeply protected in underground fortification on the east bank.

Israel replied by bombing attacks not only on the guns and other military installations but also on civilian targets deep in Egypt.

The Big Four powers in the Security Council—the United States, the U.S.S.R., the United Kingdom and France—in an effort to hasten a peaceful settlement and prevent a resumption of full-scale war which might involve them, began to hold meetings in New York for the purpose of developing a peace formula to be presented to the combatants. Israel promptly warned that it would not accept an "imposed settlement." Washington as promptly assured her that there was no intention to do that.

Months passed during which meeting after meeting was held, but no agreement was reached, and the idea was dropped.

In the spring of 1970, United States Secretary of State William P. Rogers decided to try his hand at peacemaking. He proposed a cease-fire for ninety days during which negotiations for peace would be intensified. Both Egypt and Israel agreed, and a new cease-fire took effect August 7, 1970. Although this cease-fire was extended twice, no agreement was reached. Dr. Jarring's patient and persevering efforts collapsed because Israel consistently refused to even promise withdrawal from the occupied territories.

President Nasser of Egypt died in September 1970. His

successor, Anwar Sadat, quickly announced that he was willing to continue the negotiations through Ambassador Jarring, who had returned to his post at Moscow very much discouraged.

In February 1971, as a last resort, Ambassador Jarring decided to force the parties to lay their cards on the table. He addressed to them separate aide memoirs in which he asked specific questions concerning their willingness to comply with the various provisions of Security Council Resolution 242 approved in November 1967 and until then still unimplemented.

Egypt's reply was considered satisfactory. Israel's was not. For one thing, it said flatly: Israel will not withdraw to the pre-June 5, 1967, lines. The Israelis also wondered whether the United Nations Special Representative had any right to ask specific questions.

This rebuff caused Jarring to give up any hope of success. He returned to his post in Moscow as Swedish ambassador.

In May 1971, United States Secretary of State Rogers, hoping that he could persuade the parties to reach a political settlement, visited Tel Aviv and Cairo. He attempted to push the opening of the Suez Canal. While both Egypt and Israel expressed their approval of the idea, they could not agree on the terms, and the secretary's mission failed.

Rogers, by the way, became *persona non grata* to Israel when he said that the United States opposed Israeli retention of the occupied Arab territories but would support some border adjustments that "did not reflect the weight of conquest." When he later resigned, Henry Kissinger, who had been running U.S. foreign policy from the White House, succeeded him.

To enable Israel to survive economically during the years of no peace, no war, which followed the 1967 war, the United States has been pouring hundreds of millions of dollars annually into her coffers. And the Pentagon, on orders of the

White House, has kept up the flow of jets, tanks, and other weapons of offensive warfare into Tel Aviv.

So peace remained only a hope.

As long as the United States is willing to finance Israel's wars and assure her military superiority, what is the incentive for her to evacuate the occupied Arab territory?

XIV

The Internal Arab Situation

Israel's 1967 lightning victory over the Arabs, with such heavy losses in men, machines, and territories, was thought by the Israelis and others to be great enough to force the Arabs to their knees. But soon this Israeli hope evaporated.

At an Arab summit meeting held at Khartoum in September 1967, the assembled heads of Arab states issued a defiant statement in which they said that they had agreed that there will be "no negotiations, no recognition and no peace" with Israel. As we have seen, Egypt and Jordan in 1971 committed themselves to end the state of belligerency and recognize Israel in return for the evacuation of their territories and a just settlement of the Palestinian refugees problem. Obviously, this is a retreat from the Khartoum manifesto.

Although immediately after the cease-fire in 1967 Russia undertook to rearm the defense forces of Egypt and Syria and also sent thousands of Russian troops to both countries to train their armies, these armies were still incapable of mounting an offensive in 1972, five years after the war. So to express his displeasure and to open the door for America, President Sadat of Egypt ordered the Soviet military advisers out of his country in July 1972. They left promptly. So Egypt lost the services of these men. But Washington ignored the opportunity.

Jordan was left in worse shape militarily. King Hussein, taking his cues from Washington, had been adamant about dealing with the Soviet Union, which offered to equip his army. And while Washington had given him some Skyhawk jets and also some tanks, his army remained incapable of making a stand against the Israeli forces, much less join in an offensive operation. Hussein frankly stated in late 1972 that not only Jordan but all the Arabs were still incapable of waging a successful war against Israel, and that should war come, he would not allow himself to be "dragged" into it.

Aware of their weaknesses, Egypt and Syria remained quiet but kept on bolstering their defenses. As late as 1969 when President Nasser started his "war of attrition," it was felt that Egypt could stop an Israeli advance on land but could not mount an offensive. Nor could it cope with Israeli air raids. Syria was in a similar position.

The Palestinians, who had started the chain of events that culminated in the Six Day War, refused to remain quiet. They increased their attacks along Israel's border with Jordan. Israel retaliated with air raids.

In March 1968, Israel decided to put an end to these attacks, which kept Israeli citizens on edge although they did little real harm. A tank column crossed the Jordan River and attacked the town of Karameh, which housed 25,000 Palestinian refugees. They demolished the whole town and spread death and destruction everywhere. The Palestinians fought back and fought well, to the surprise of the Israelis and to the delight of the Arabs. So did Jordan's army. The retreating attackers left behind them several vehicles, including tanks, one of which was driven to Amman by King Hussein. But the Israelis took with them close to two hundred prisoners—men whom they suspected of being commandos.

The battle of Karameh became a turning point in Arab psychology. It proved, said some editorials, that the Israelis were not nine feet tall and that they could be beaten by Arab fighting men.

Karameh was still deserted when this writer visited it in the spring of 1969 and again in 1972. But the anniversary of "the battle of Karameh" was being commemorated all over the Arab world with patriotic songs and speeches and generous contributions to Al Fateh, the guerilla group that claimed credit for "the victory."

Whether justified or not, the battle of Karameh lifted up Arab spirits, enhanced the prestige of the Palestinian resistance forces, and caused thousands of young men to seek enlistment in Al Fateh, including many who thought it profitable to join the ranks of this now very popular organization. Amman swarmed with young men wearing the camouflage fatigues of the commandos. And so did Damascus. Money, too, poured into the coffers of Al Fateh and the other commando groups. King Hussein's authority in Jordan's capital and other towns began to be threatened.

Yasser Arafat, the leader of Al Fateh, began to be talked about as a great Arab leader, and an "audience" with him was soon to be considered a great honor. He became a legend.

Another guerilla leader, Dr. George Habash, whose small organization once hijacked three airliners in one day and had two of them land in Jordan and then defied the Jordan government to obtain their release, likewise became a great hero.

But the success and prestige of the guerillas proved their undoing. King Hussein felt that he was being overshadowed by Arafat, and Habash's defiant attitude got under his skin.

So King Hussein, with the encouragement of Washington and to the delight of Israel, in September 1970 declared war on the Palestinian guerilla organizations. His Bedouin army used tanks and field guns against them, inflicting heavy casualties on them and also on the civilian population of Amman. At least one Palestinian refugee camp near Amman was attacked by Jordanian army tanks, killing many persons.

This war was resumed in 1971 until Jordan was cleared of Palestinian guerillas.

When Syria attempted to intervene on the side of the Palestinians, the American Sixth Fleet, reinforced by several units, including another carrier, began to move toward the eastern Mediterranean shores, and American arms poured into Amman by air.

Israeli forces also began to move toward the cease-fire line with Syria.

President Nasser and other Arab leaders attempted to bring about an understanding between Hussein and the guerillas but failed. Consequently, Egypt, Iraq, and Syria broke diplomatic relations with Amman and closed their borders with Jordan. Nasser was saddened. Soon afterward he died of a heart attack.

Libya and Kuwait, which had been paying Jordan a subsidy to help it maintain its army, stopped payment. Libya's leader, Colonel Muammar Qaddafi declared publicly that Hussein must go. But Hussein remains.

The action of these countries evidently had serious effect on Jordan's economy and forced King Hussein in the latter part of 1971 to seek assistance from President Nixon, stating that unless aid is received promptly, Jordan might resort to *Ghazou* (raid). But one wonders what country or what city he would raid.

Late in 1972, Jordan was still a country under siege, with little contact with the outside world. Ironically, the only foreign air line operating from or to the Amman International Airport was the Russian Aeroflot. Syria permitted no other airline to use its air space to or from Jordan.

Nasser's death in September 1970 was felt by Arabs everywhere. Many now asked "whither Egypt," the most populous and most powerful Arab state. But the election of Anwar Sadat—Nasser's long-time comrade—as president and his announcement of a policy along the lines followed by his illustrious predecessor soon reassured them.

It so happens that President Nasser died of a heart attack while President Nixon was reviewing Sixth Fleet maneuvers in the eastern Mediterranean, intended no doubt to impress the Russians and also Nasser and his Arab followers. A question was soon being whispered as to whether these maneuvers and Nixon's presence in those waters contributed to Nasser's frustrations and his heart attack.

President Sadat of Egypt announced that 1972 was "a year of decision" between war and peace, and if no peaceful settlement was reached, Egypt would be forced to fight to recover its territory. His foreign minister, Mahmoud Riad, was reported on December 31, 1971, as stating that the Egyptian forces were now ready for war. Israel's military leaders promptly challenged Cairo to start it.

On the same date, Israel's Prime Minister Golda Meir stated that Washington had decided to supply her country with more Phantom fighter-bomber jets.

"Is President Nixon trying to push Sadat into war?" asked one Egyptian journalist. Perhaps Nixon was trying to discourage war. But more arms for Israel have not encouraged a peaceful settlement either.

XV

The October War

Six years elapsed, and Security Council Resolution 242, adopted in November 1967, remained unimplemented. Arab demands for the evacuation of their occupied territories were answered by the Israeli leaders with a demand for face-to-face negotiations and the signing of a "contractual agreement" giving Israel "secure boundaries." At the same time these leaders said they would not give up Arab Jerusalem, would not evacuate Sharm al-Sheikh, and also maintained that the Golan Heights, where a score of Israeli settlements had been established, were part of Israel and would never be returned to Syria. They also asserted that Israel intended to keep a military garrison along the west bank of the Jordan River.

The Arabs regarded these demands as tantamount to a demand for surrender, which they were not ready to do. So the state of no war, no peace continued to exist.

In the meantime, the Suez Canal remained closed at a great loss to Egypt and the world.

Israel, however, enjoyed a great prosperity. Tourism boomed. New immigrants arrived daily in ever greater numbers. Money poured in from public and private sources in the United States. The Egyptian oil fields in Sinai were exploited to the fullest, thus saving Tel Aviv hundreds of millions in hard currency annually.

Israel felt more secure than ever before. Obviously the Suez Canal and the Jordan River were better borders from a military standpoint. And King Hussein's expulsion of the Palestinian commandos from Jordan gave her a respite from their incursions. Syria no longer commanded the Golan Heights. Israel had no incentive to seek peace. But she shied from annexing the "new territories," as many Israelis called them. They contained over a million Arabs, and with over 400,000 already in pre-1967 Israel, the Arabs would constitute over one third of the state's total population. And because of their higher birthrate, they are likely to become a majority within a few decades.

Fear of being thus submerged by the Arabs caused many Israelis to advocate evacuation of these territories, the retention of which required the maintenance of a huge military establishment which kept the Tel Aviv treasury broke.

The Religious Party leaders, however, said it would be a sin to give up any part of "Eretz Israel." This argument applied especially to the West Bank, where the bulk of these Arabs lived.

The Likud Party also objected to withdrawal.

Unable to agree on a policy, Israel followed the expedient policy of simply resisting peace. Arab threats to fight to recover their territories were met by the threat to inflict upon them "a more crushing defeat than the 1967 defeat."

These threats and counterthreats were ignored by Washington, which held the key to peace and war. Even the ousting on July 18, 1972, of the thousands of Soviet military advisers from Egypt did not create much of a ripple in Washington.

This writer was in Tel Aviv on that day and learned about this event, which constituted a great turning point in Egyptian policy, from the political officer of the American embassy there who was greatly excited hours before the news broke on the radio that day. Needless to say, this momentous step created great excitement in Israel and raised many questions in the Arab world. But it met with utter silence in Washington.

Upon his return to the United States, the writer, who had gone to the Middle East for the second time since the 1967 war to gauge the chances for peace and search for a fair and acceptable peace formula, told the Department of State that his conversations in Israel and in some of the Arab states had led him to believe that the time was propitious for the United States to start a peace drive, if not at once, then immediately after the elections. The elections came, and Richard M. Nixon was reelected and inaugurated for a second term. But no attempt was made to tackle the Middle East problem, although the White House did promise Jordan a move for peace immediately after the elections.

Then the Watergate affair took a new twist, which claimed priority on Nixon's time. The Middle East was forgotten.

The United Nations proved to be helpless. Its numerous resolutions were simply ignored by Israel. Steps to compel compliance with them were frustrated by Washington, which in July 1973, for the first time, used its veto power not to promote a peaceful settlement but to support Israel's intransigent policy. The occasion was a resolution supported by thirteen of the fifteen-member Security Council, calling upon Israel to withdraw from the occupied territories and condemning her for rejecting the peace proposals.[17]

In the meantime, Washington continued to make certain of an "arms balance"—in favor of Israel.

While the Arabs time and again won the support of the world peace organization and many solemn resolutions were adopted against Israel, this support meant little or nothing.

Giving up all hope of regaining their territories peacefully, the Arabs finally decided to fight for them. In late September 1973, Egyptian and Syrian ground forces began to move toward the fronts. Tanks and materiel for pontoon bridges piled up along the Suez Canal. The Israeli intelligence organi-

---

17. The U.S. has since used or threatened to use the veto a dozen times in behalf of Israel.

zation watched these moves and reported them to Tel Aviv. But General Dayan and the general staff shrugged off the reports. The Arabs must be conducting a maneuver, they thought.

On October 5, an Israeli defense-ministry spokesman casually reported "increasing tension along the Suez and Golan cease-fire lines." *Maariv,* the large-circulation Israeli daily newspaper, stated that Israeli troops were watching the activities of the Egyptians west of the Suez Canal and that measures had been taken to prevent them from launching any military operation. General Dayan issued his usual challenge and repeated his dire threats.

The American press paid little attention to the movement of the Arab forces. It was apparently thought that these movements were only a bluff by President Sadat to force reactivation of peace talks. No one believed that he would dare start a "suicidal" war.

To launch a full-scale war across the Suez Canal and challenge the Israelis in their underground fortifications was truly a formidable task for any army.

To throw bridges over the canal under fire is a dangerous enough operation but not an impossible one. The problem was how to land and move on the ground after reaching the east side of the canal. For on the east bank there was a thick and very high sand wall that challenged man and machine to negotiate it. And behind this was the "impregnable" Bar-Lev Line.[18]

Besides, the Arab states had not been in the habit of starting war against Israel. Their leaders often threatened to do so but never dared carry out their threats. In both the 1956 and the 1967 wars, it was Israel that attacked first. Would the Arabs, after their 1967 crushing defeat, dare start war now? Nonsense. The movement of the troops was only a maneuver. Indeed, so thought the Egyptian troops themselves while marching toward the Suez Canal. They did not know that they

18. These fortifications were shown on U.S. television, presumably to convince Americans that the ingenious Israelis were on the bank of the Suez Canal to stay.

were going to war until the order was given to cross the canal.

This time, sufficiently trained, they unhesitatingly responded. Over quickly erected bridges and in rubber boats, the sons of the Nile swarmed into Sinai. The "impregnable" Bar-Lev Line was stormed, to the surprise of its garrison, who had thought that they were perfectly safe there.

When early on that October Saturday morning (October 6) a CBS newsman in New York telephoned this writer to inform him of the war and ask for his comment, he could hardly believe what had happened and inquired if this was not only a commando action. (He had seen the "Chinese wall" on the east bank and knew how difficult it would be to cross it.) But the newsman replied that it was a full-scale war, that thousands of Egyptian troops and scores of tanks were already on the east side of the canal, and more were pouring in.

The Egyptian crossing of the canal and their occupation of the Bar-Lev Line constituted a great feat, which won them the respect of people everywhere.

How did the Egyptian army cross the canal and move through the high and seemingly impenetrable wall on the east bank? Their biggest guns and their most powerful tanks had proved helpless before similar parapets erected for tests. The answer was simple. According to their commander, General Shazly, the weapon they used so effectively to breach them was water. Yes, water. Streams of water under high pressure caused the sand to cave in and run down, thus opening a breach for tanks and troops to go through. One hundred high pressure pumps, each spouting one thousand gallons of water per minute melted the parapets. Some infantry units, who had crossed over on the pontoons or in boats, climbed to the top of the parapets on the ladders built for that purpose.

The Syrians on the north attacked simultaneously. They quickly overran the Golan district, which was occupied by Israel in 1967, and threatened Israeli settlements west of the 1949 armistice line.

The Israelis, to prevent an invasion of their own territory, concentrated their efforts against Syria and soon drove the

Syrians back beyond the 1967 cease-fire line but at a high price. A wounded Syrian tank commander speaking from his hospital bed said: "I have no regrets about being here. I destroyed five Israeli tanks before I was hit." But the fact remains that Arab losses were heavy. Unable to defeat the Syrian troops on the battlefield, Israel started to attack Syria's cities and industries. Damascus and other cities were attacked. Refineries, power stations, and factories were destroyed. "Bomb them back to the stone age," said an Israeli spokesman.

Israeli losses on both fronts were much heavier than the Israelis had been accustomed to. Egyptian and Syrian anti-aircraft defenses were more effective than in the previous wars. Israel's air superiority, heretofore depended upon to defeat the Arabs, was more or less neutralized. When two armies are engaged in close-range combat or hand-to-hand fighting, air power cannot be used against the enemy.

Israel, with a population of less than three million, could not stand heavy losses in men. Moreover, a third of the Israeli tank force was destroyed during the first week of the war. The economic damage of the war was great, especially to Israel. The Israeli pound was devalued in 1974 from four pounds to six pounds to the dollar. In June 1975, an additional 2 percent devaluation was announced in Jerusalem. Despite the fact that Arab losses were much heavier, Tel Aviv became gloomy. Defeat, previously unknown to Israelis, now stared them in the face. But not for long.

President Nixon and Secretary of State Henry Kissinger sprang to Israel's rescue. They mounted an airlift of jets, tanks, and electronic gear, valued at more than two billion dollars, which enabled the Jewish troops to continue to fight and even to threaten to win against the Arabs. Objections by the Department of Defense to this massive transfer of sophisticated weapons, which left some American units short, were ignored by Kissinger, who had no difficulty winning the backing of the president against the Pentagon. The arrival of these arms caused Egyptian President Sadat to cry in anguish, "I cannot fight the United States."

The transportation of these weapons did not contribute to better relations between us and our European allies. The latter objected to the use of their countries for the massive American airlift. They insisted that they were neutral in this war and correctly maintained that the use of their airfields or air space violates their neutrality. Secretary of State Henry Kissinger publicly expressed his displeasure with this European attitude.

The chasm between the United States and Western Europe widened considerably when early on October 25, President Nixon, without consulting our NATO allies, alerted America's armed forces everywhere and thus brought the world to the brink of a nuclear conflagration. The reason for this action was not stated. People are still wondering why such a momentous step was taken. The United States had announced on October 7 that an agreement had been rached with the Soviet Union and China to limit the war and prevent it from spreading. But now, on October 25, three days after the U.N. Security Council had, at our request, ordered a cease-fire, Washington alerted its mighty forces, stationed throughout the world, for a global war.

The Nixon administration never pretended to be neutral or "even handed" in this war. When Secretary Kissinger received the news of the Egyptian crossing of the Suez Canal, he became alarmed about Israel's safety and promptly notified the president, who was relaxing at his Florida home.

Immediately, four warships, including the aircraft carrier *Independence,* were ordered to proceed from Athens to the eastern Mediterranean, obviously to help Israel if she needed help. These were followed by the *Roosevelt* and the *Kennedy* and also some helicopter carriers loaded with marines.

It had long been known that one of the primary tasks of our Sixth Fleet in the Mediterranean was the defense of Israel. Back in 1965, Zionist Walt Rostow, national security adviser to President Lyndon Johnson (the position later held by Henry

Kissinger under President Richard M. Nixon before Kissinger became secretary of state) formally assured Israel that the Sixth Fleet would come to its aid whenever it needed aid.[19]

Naval officers, appearing before the Appropriation Committee of the House of Representatives to ask for larger budgets, have pleaded "the defense of Israel" to justify their requests.

Now the surprising performance of the Egyptian soldier on the Suez Canal front, although far away from Israel, seemed to pose a threat. So units of the Sixth Fleet, as well as the Atlantic fleet, were ordered to move closer.

On October 7, the United States called for a meeting of the Security Council. When the Council met the next day, Ambassador Scali called for an end to the fighting and a return to the lines held before the war started. This was rejected by the members. It will be recalled that in the 1967 war, the United States opposed a cease-fire resolution that included a demand for Israeli withdrawal from Arab territory occupied by her forces. This time the United States wanted Egypt, whose troops were still on their own soil, to retreat and thus force Egypt back to the west bank of the Suez Canal.

When Israel failed to crush the Arabs in six days as it did in 1967, Secretary Kissinger warned that a prolonged war in the Middle East would create "a high possibility of great power involvement," and the supply of arms to Israel was speeded up to prevent—it was explained—"the massive airlift by the Soviets from unsettling the military balance in the area." Translated, this meant to assure an Israeli victory.

On October 9, President Nixon asked the Congress for $2.2 billion aid to Israel for the purchase of arms. His request for this huge sum was approved. Nixon did this while he, in the

---

19. While Walt Rostow controlled America's foreign policy at the White House, his brother Eugene Rostow held its reins at the Department of State. Both are Zionists.

name of economy in government, was withholding funds voted by Congress for social services at home.

In response to this American policy, the oil-exporting Arab states announced a reduction of oil production. This was followed by an embargo of oil shipments to the United States.

The president and the secretary of state asserted that the oil embargo was intolerable, that it had disrupted industry and created additional unemployment, which the world would not and should not permit. There were threats of retaliation and even hints at occupying the Arab oil fields. As it was known that some U.S. forces had already been trained for desert warfare, the Arabs replied that in case of invasion they would blow up the oil wells and the pipelines. It was also stated that some of these installations had already been wired, ready to go up at the flick of a switch.

Actually, however, the Arab oil embargo was lifted before it had any serious effect on the energy crisis in the United States, which began years earlier and is still with us today. Europe and Japan are largely dependent on Arab oil, but not the United States. Most of our imported oil comes from Canada and Venezuela.

President Nixon apparently did not know about President Johnson's refusal in the '60s to sell wheat to Egypt when that country was faced with famine because of poor harvest while the United States was trying to find ways to dispose of a two-year surplus of wheat. No one here called that action "illegal" or "intolerable." Neither Nixon nor Ford lifted the blockade against Cuba, imposed following the establishment of the Castro regime there two decades ago. They also seem to have forgotten our "Trading with the Enemy Act" and our trade policy toward Red China prior to 1972.

Nixon's chosen successor, Gerald Ford, a known strong Zionist, talked much as Nixon had. Of course, both presidents took their cues from Kissinger.

According to Kissinger, Russia, whose relations with Egypt had cooled off following the expulsion of the Soviet military

97

advisers, attempted to stage a comeback and speeded up the shipment of arms to the Arabs. This naturally alarmed Kissinger who, before becoming secretary of state, had stated that his policy's goal was the eviction of Russia from the Middle East. But his fears were not justified, because Sadat soon was complaining that the Soviets were not supplying Egypt with arms and began to shop elsewhere to replace the arms lost during the October war. And early in 1976 Egypt abrogated its treaty of friendship with Moscow.

After a quick visit to Moscow by Kissinger, the United States and Russia called for a meeting of the Security Council and submitted the following cease-fire resolution, which was approved on October 22:

The Security Council:
1. Calls upon all parties to the present fighting to cease all firing and terminate all military activity immediately, no later than 12 hours after the moment of the adoption of this decision in the positions they now occupy.
2. Calls upon the parties concerned to start immediately after the cease-fire the implementation of Security Council Resolution 242 in all of its parts.
3. Decides that immediately and concurrently with the cease-fire, negotiations start between the parties concerned under appropriate auspices aimed at establishing a just and durable peace in the Middle East.

The resolution was immediately accepted by both Egypt and Israel. But fighting continued.

The Israeli troops, unable to push the Egyptians back across the canal, had managed to cross it themselves prior to October 22, thus driving a wedge between the Egyptian Second and Third Armies on the east side of the canal. Now they wanted to reinforce their bridgehead on the west bank of the canal and consolidate their position there. So they ignored the cease-fire order and proceeded to cut the supply line of the

Egyptian Third Army, which held the southern end of the fighting line. They succeeded in reaching and holding the city of Suez, and thus they cut the Suez-Cairo road on which both the city and the Third Army received their supplies from Cairo. The situation became critical for both sides. Egypt's Third Army was now almost surrounded by the enemy. And so was the Israeli force west of the canal. This unusual situation inspired the following headline in a leading American daily: "Egypt, Israel, Completely Beseiged."

Of course, neither country was besieged. And neither army was completely cut off from its source of supply.

Egypt complained that Israel had violated the cease-fire resolution and that its occupation of the city of Suez was illegal. The Security Council, on October 23, adopted a second resolution that repeated the cease-fire order and called upon Israel to withdraw to the line held on October 22.

Fighting stopped following the second Security Council resolution. But Israel refused to withdraw to the October 22 line. Israel's Prime Minister Golda Meir said she did not know where that line was. It was then that United States Secretary of State Kissinger began his now famous "shuttle diplomacy." He quickly induced Egypt and Israel to agree to a disengagement of their forces, which was signed at Geneva in the presence of United States and Soviet representatives.

This agreement called for Israeli withdrawal not only from the area west of the Suez Canal but also to a line a few miles east of it. It also created a buffer zone between the two armies which has been occupied by U.N. troops.

Despite his intervention with that massive arms airlift to Israel, which robbed the Arabs of victory, Kissinger soon won the friendship of President Sadat of Egypt. The latter began to refer to our secretary of state as "my friend" and "brother" and they embraced and kissed each time they met. Sadat also expressed admiration for President Nixon while the latter was facing impeachment.

Kissinger and Nixon, in turn, asked the Congress to appropriate 250 million dollars for Egypt to rebuild the cities on the banks of the Suez Canal, which had been destroyed by Israel during the 1967 war and the 1969 to 1970 "war of attrition." Now Israel wanted them rebuilt and repopulated to become hostages against a resumption of war by Egypt.

Sadat reestablished diplomatic relations with Washington, which were severed during the 1967 war. And, as his relations with Washington warmed up, he became increasingly critical of Russia, which, for two decades, had been Egypt's principal source of arms and technical and economic assistance.

The war in the Golan area also stopped pursuant to the Security Council's orders. But soon it started again on a limited scale. Artillery and tank firings were exchanged daily for nearly three months for control of Mount Hermon's peak, which both sides wanted for strategic purposes.

Securing a disengagement of forces between Israel and Syria proved to be a very difficult task even for the now legendary diplomat, and "miracle worker." It took Dr. Kissinger thirty-three days of continuous shuttling between Israel, Syria, and Egypt (a record for an American secretary of state to be outside the United States). But he finally wrung an agreement which was signed in Geneva on May 31, 1974. His perseverance paid off.

Like the agreement between Israel and Egypt, the Syrian agreement created a buffer zone to be occupied by U.N. troops and called for a thinning out of forces on each side of it. It also required Israel to withdraw from the Golan's principal city, Al-Kuneitra, which was made a heap of rubble before the Israelis withdrew from it.

Al-Kuneitra did not return to Syria's military control because it is located in the U.N. buffer zone. When Kissinger returned to Washington, he spoke of a hundred-million-dollar grant to Syria for rebuilding it.

Syria, too, reestablished diplomatic relations with the United States, which were broken during the Six Day War.

Upon Kissinger's triumphant return to Washington, Presi-

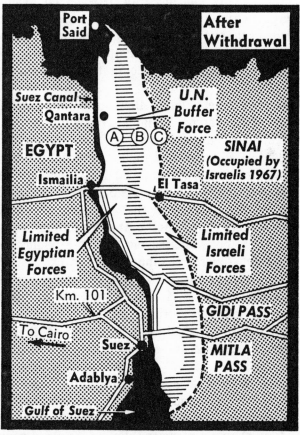

First Egyptian-Israeli disengagement lines.

dent Nixon announced that he would make a visit to several Arab states and to Israel beginning June 9. The exact purpose of this visit was not stated. It is assumed, however, that he wanted to promote a final settlement of the long-standing Arab-Israeli war or at least reassure the Arabs—and Israel also—of America's good intentions toward them both.

Those already convinced of Nixon's complicity in the Watergate cover-up and other charges could see nothing in this trip, or the one to Moscow which followed, but an attempt to improve his image and divert attention from the soon-to-be-announced House Judiciary Committee's decision to impeach him.

One cannot help noting that during his visits to Cairo, Jedda, and Damascus, President Nixon talked of economics and technology though President Sadat, King Faisal, and President Assad talked of Israeli withdrawal and the rights of the Palestinians. As Mohammed Hassanein Heykal was reported to have told the *Christian Science Monitor* later, "Mr. Nixon did not understand that the great crowds that welcomed him meant not that the Arab world was asking him for economic aid but was receiving him on a political note—the demand for American support in solving the Palestinian problem." Heykal, the well-known former editor of the leading Arab world newspaper, *Al Ahram,* evidently assumed that the evacuation of Arab territory occupied by Israel in 1967, especially Egypt's Sinai, was assured and that the main problem to be solved at Geneva was that of Palestine and the Palestinians.

In March 1975, to postpone another Geneva meeting at which the Russians would have to be present, and to separate Egypt from her Arab world partners, Kissinger made another round of "shuttle diplomacy." He made several trips between Egypt and Israel for the purpose of obtaining another Israeli withdrawal from Egypt's Sinai. But Israel demanded "non-belligerency" as the price for a substantial withdrawal that would return the strategic Mitla and Gidi passes and the Abu

Rudeis oil field to Egypt. President Sadat rejected this demand, and Kissinger returned empty-handed—and tearful. Despite this rebuff by Israel, according to the *Washington Post* of March 26, he told a closed-door meeting of the House Foreign Affairs Committee that "the United States could not permit Israel to be defeated should war break out in the Middle East."

Nevertheless, the failure of the Kissinger effort caused President Ford to order a "reassessment" of American policy in the Middle East.

In the meantime, President Sadat won another diplomatic victory against Israel by announcing early in April that he would agree to an extension of the U.N. force's mandate in the buffer zone between Egypt and Israel for an additional three months, and, to help the world economic situation (and also help Egypt), he would reopen the Suez Canal on June 5, 1975, the eighth anniversary of the 1967 war. He did.

President Assad of Syria quickly followed Sadat's example and said he would extend the U.N. mandate in his country so that its end would coincide with that in Egypt.

As we have seen, the conflict started in Palestine over that country's control and the right of its inhabitants to continue to live in it and, if not to rule it, to have a part in ruling it. Let us, therefore, examine both sides' claims to Palestine.

XVI

The Palestinians' Claim To Palestine

The Palestinians' claim is predicated on the right of ownership evidenced by uninterrupted possession and occupation since the dawn of recorded history. They lived in the country when the Hebrews (of whom the Jews claim descent) came and lived there for a comparatively short period. They continued to live there during the Hebrew (and Jewish) occupation. They remained there after the last Hebrew or Jew left the country nearly two thousand years ago. And at the time of the latest Jewish invasion, through immigration under the protection of British guns, the Palestinians were still in Palestine and owned its farmland, orchards, cities, towns, and villages. This ownership was shown on the land records of the country when Israel was established there.

Between the birth of the Zionist movement in the closing years of the nineteenth century and the proclamation of the State of Israel in 1948, the Jews were able to acquire the ownership of only 6 percent of Palestine's total area. Yet this new state comprised 80 percent of it.

It is deemed advisable here to define the terms *Palestinians,* or *Palestinian Arabs,* and give the origin of the people they describe.

The people today called *Palestinians* or *Palestinian Arabs,* who have been fighting the Zionists and the State of Israel which Zionism created in 1948, are largely the descendants of the Canaanites, the Edomites, and the Philistines who lived in Palestine when it was invaded by the Hebrews in ancient times. But the Hebrews finally left or were driven out two thousand years ago.

The Canaanites were, like the Hebrews, a Semitic Arab tribe that settled in Palestine over five thousand years ago. They were already well established there when, according to the Bible, Abraham, the ancestor of the Hebrews (and many of the Arab tribes), migrated to the country some four thousand years ago. Abraham had to ask permission from Melchizedek, the king of Jerusalem, to pitch his tent and graze his livestock in the "Land of Canaan."

The Philistines, who occupied the coastal plains of the country which has borne their name for centuries, are a people who appear to have come from some of the Aegean islands. Their racial origin has been in doubt. But recent discoveries suggest that they were a part of the Canaanite tribe or nation that, after leaving Arabia, continued its trek westward, sailed to the Aegean islands, lived there for some time, returned to the mainland, and settled along the Mediterranean coast of Palestine. This reverse migration took place before the time of Abraham, as it is shown elsewhere in this work.

When the Hebrews invaded the country in the twelfth century B.C. under the leadership of Moses and Joshua, the Canaanites and the Philistines had a highly developed civilization with a well-organized agricultural and commercial economy. According to the Bible, the Hebrew invaders killed thousands of the inhabitants and despoiled other thousands in a war that lasted over a century. During this period, they succeeded in subduing only a small part of the country, that which is known today as Jordan's West Bank plus the eastern part of Galilee. Even this part was not completely emptied of its Canaanite population.

Among the Palestinians of today must be included the

descendants of the Edomites, who occupied the part of Palestine south of Gaza and Beersheba. According to the Bible, the Edomites were the children of Edom, or Essau, the son of Isaac and the brother of Jacob, the ancestor of the Jews and the other eleven tribes of Israel.

The land of Edom, or Idumea, as the Romans called it, was not occupied by Joshua, and the Edomites later merged with the Canaanites and the Philistines. Its occupation was forbidden by God, who told Moses that he would not give him "one foot" of the land of Edom.

We must also include the Jews who became Christians or Muslims. As the reader knows, the first Christians were Jews. The disciples of Jesus were Jews, and Christianity was regarded as a Jewish sect, or a Jewish reform movement. The descendants of these Jews are today Palestinians, or Palestinian Arabs.

Likewise, the descendants of the Greek and Roman families who came to Palestine and remained there after the end of the Greco-Roman rule today are an indivisible part of the Palestinian people.

The greatest and most lasting transformation of the population of Palestine occurred in the seventh century A.D., when the armies of Islam came and freed Palestine and the entire Middle East of Roman rule. The Palestinians, then still speaking Aramaic, found little difficulty in changing over to the Arabic of the Koran. Indeed, thousands of them converted to Islam.

We must also include in the term *Palestinians* the descendants of the European families who came with the crusaders during the tenth and eleventh centuries A.D. and remained in the country after the victorious Arabs drove the last crusader out of the Holy Land.

These are the Palestinian people who lived in Palestine until 1948, when the state of Israel was established and 80 percent of them were driven out of their homes and country and have since lived in the United Nations camps in Jordan, Syria, and

Lebanon as "refugees," totally dependent upon international charity for their sustenance.

Beaten in the war of 1948, dispossessed and driven out of their homes and country, and living under extremely miserable and humiliating conditions since that time, they still stoutly claim the right to go back, and they refuse to recognize the legitimacy of the State of Israel or the right of the Jews to the country.

Most of them hoped and still hope that the international community would take the necessary steps to achieve their repatriation. Some have become tired and weary of waiting and, despairing of obtaining justice by remaining quiet and peaceful, have resorted to violence against Israel, despite the obvious great odds against them. And for doing this they have been called "terrorists." But the Arab world calls them *fedayeen*, i.e., men ready to sacrifice themselves in pursuit of their rights. In this suicidal struggle, they have so far been the losers. Yet they refuse to give up.

About 85 percent of the Palestinian Arabs are Muslims. The rest are Christians. The Israeli army that wrested control of the country from them made no distinction between the Muslims and the Christians. They attacked both without regard to their religion. So the refugees are both Christians and Muslims. So are the fedayeen.

XVII

The Zionists' Claim

From time to time, the Zionists have advanced different arguments in support of the establishment of a Jewish state in Palestine. These arguments are:

    1. the religious argument, which is, in effect, that God promised to give Palestine to the Jews; this promise was made to their ancestors—Abraham, Isaac, and Jacob—as recorded in the Bible;

    2. the "statelessness" of the Jews, a people without a country, and that they should have one in which to live, practice their religion, and develop their own culture; and that since they once lived in Palestine, they should be allowed to return to it;

    3. that the Balfour Declaration of 1917 granted them Palestine, and this grant was confirmed by the League of Nations;

    4. that the United Nations granted them the right in 1947 to establish a Jewish state in Palestine.

Let us study these arguments in the order listed above.

XVIII

The "Promised Land" Argument

In this age of space flights, moon exploration, and nuclear power, it seems ridiculous to discuss the merits of a claim by a group of foreign persons to a country on the grounds that some four thousand years ago God promised it to them. But the claim is based on passages in the Bible, which are read and believed not only by Zionists and other Jews but also by Christians and which are quoted in Sunday morning sermons by thousands of Christian ministers and read to children in Sunday schools and to adult Bible classes in thousands of parishes every week. This has caused some people to believe and assert that the establishment of the state of Israel in 1948 is a fulfillment of God's four thousand-year-old promise.

Besides, in his book *The Birth and Destiny of Israel*, David Ben-Gurion, Israel's first prime minister, said that the Bible gives the Jews a "sacrosanct title-deed to Palestine."

For these reasons it is deemed necessary to discuss this claim fully, and in doing so we shall restrict ourselves to the words of the Bible. Because it is the most widely read, we shall use the King James edition unless otherwise indicated.

The book of Genesis, which contains the material in question, says that the promise was originally made to Abram in Haran, Syria, after his father, Terah, brought the family

109

from Ur of the Chaldees to go to the land of Canaan, but Terah decided to stay in Haran, where he died (Gen. 11:31-32). Shortly after Terah's death, the Lord appeared to Abram and said, "Get thee out of thy country, and from thy kindred, and from thy father's house, unto a land that I will shew thee" (Gen. 12:1).

Abram, in obedience to this command, folded up his tent, took his wife Sarai, his nephew Lot, and their flocks and shepherds and proceeded by stages to Palestine, finally pitching tents in the plain of Moreh near Sichem. Here God appeared to him again and said, "Unto thy seed will I give this land" (Gen. 12:7).

Abram did not remain in this area very long. He moved southward and, because of a drought that caused famine in Palestine, went down to Egypt. He was expelled from that country when it was discovered that he had falsely told the Egyptians that Sarai was his sister. It seems that Sarai was so beautiful that the Pharaoh decided to marry her. As was the custom, he bestowed lavish gifts upon Abram. Pharaoh, discovering the truth, returned Sarai to Abram and ordered him out of the country but let him keep the gifts he had given him. So Abram returned to Palestine richer than when he had left it.

Abraham (his name had been changed from Abram to Abraham) repeated this unmanly performance at Gerar and led Abimelech, king of Gerar, to take Sarah (Sarai) for a wife. Before touching her, however, the Lord appeared to Abimelech in a dream and told him that the woman had a husband. Abimelech pleaded his innocence, and early the next morning summoned Abraham and demanded, "What possessed you to do this?" Abraham replied, "I thought there would be no fear of God here and that the people would kill me because of my wife." So Abimelech took sheep, cattle, men and women slaves, and presented them to Abraham, and gave him back his wife, plus a thousand pieces of silver.

Abimalech, who was a Philistine king, gave Abraham

permission to graze within his domain but made him swear that he would never again trick him or his descendants.

Isaac, too, represented his wife, Rebekah, as his sister in Gerar. But Abimalech discovered the truth and told his people, "whoever touches this man or his wife shall be put to death."[20]

Shortly after returning from Egypt, Abram's (Abraham's) and Lot's shepherds began to quarrel over pasture and water. To put an end to this quarrel, Abraham suggested to his nephew that they part and told him to choose the area in which he preferred to live. "And Lot lifted up his eyes and beheld all the plain of Jordan, that it was well watered every where, before the Lord destroyed Sodom and Gomorrah, even as the garden of the Lord, like the land of Egypt" (Gen. 13:10).

So Lot decided to move there. Abram (Abraham) remained in the land of Canaan.

"Abram dwelled in the land of Canaan, and Lot dwelled in the cities of the plain, and pitched his tent toward Sodom" (Gen. 13:12).

"And the Lord said unto Abram, after that Lot was separated from him, Lift up now thine eyes, and look from the place where thou art northward, and southward, and eastward, and westward:

"For all the land which thou seest, to thee will I give it, and to thy seed forever.

"And I will make thy seed as the dust of the earth: so that if a man can number the dust of the earth, then shall thy seed also be numbered.

"Arise, walk through the land in the length of it and in the breadth of it; for I will give it unto thee" (Gen. 13:14-17).

Despite God's assurance that his seed would be as numerous "as the dust of the earth," Abram complains in Gen. 15

---

20. Or was this a mistake made by the author of Genesis, attributing to Isaac what Abraham had done?

that he has no heir to inherit his estate—mostly domestic animals. So the Lord again assured him that he will have children.

> And he brought him forth abroad, and said, Look now toward heaven, and tell the stars, if thou be able to number them: and he said unto him, So shall thy seed be.
>
> And he believed in the Lord; and he counted it to him for righteousness.
>
> And he said unto him, I am the Lord that brought thee out of Ur of the Chaldees, to give thee this land to inherit it. (Gen. 15:5-7)

A few verses later on, we read, "In the same day the Lord made a covenant with Abram, saying, Unto thy seed have I given this land, from the river of Egypt unto the great river, the river Euphrates" (Gen. 15:18).[21]

But Abram still had no children, and his wife Sarai who was getting along in years and knew it, feared that the wealth they had amassed would be inherited by their steward, a man from Damascus named Eliezer. So Sarai decided that Abram should marry another woman. She chose her maid, an Egyptian named Hagar, perhaps given to her by Pharaoh, to be his second wife.

> And Sarai Abram's wife took Hagar her maid the Egyptian, after Abram had dwelt ten years in the land of Canaan, and gave her to her husband Abram to be his wife.
>
> And he went in unto Hagar, and she conceived: and when she saw that she had conceived, her mistress was despised in her eyes. (Gen. 16:3-4)

---

21. This is quite an expansion of the territory promised early that day.

Naturally enough, Sarai did not like that. And, after obtaining Abram's grudging consent, she retaliated vigorously with the result that Hagar ran away into the wilderness where an "angel of the Lord found her by a fountain of water" and said to her, "I will multiply thy seed exceedingly, that it shall not be numbered for multitude." The angel also told her that she will give birth to a son who shall be named Ishmael, who "shall dwell in the presence of all his brethren" (Gen. 16:10-13).

As ordered by the angel, Hagar returned home. In due time, she gave birth to a son, Ishmael. Abram was comforted.

Not long after Ishmael's birth, when Abram was ninety-nine years old, the Lord again appeared to him and said, "And I will give unto thee, and to thy seed after thee, the land wherein thou art a stranger, all the land of Canaan, for an everlasting possession; and I will be their God" (Gen. 17:8).

It was at this time that God made a covenant with Abram and his "seed" and ordained the rite of circumcision as "a token of the covenant betwixt me and you." Abram promptly obeyed and had himself and "every man child" in his household, including Ishmael, circumcised, for he was told that any man "not circumcised, that soul shall be cut off from his people" (Gen. 17:14). During this conversation, the Lord also told Abram that his wife Sarai will have a son, and that hence forth his name should not be Abram but Abraham, "for a father of many nations have I made thee." Sarai's name also was ordered changed to Sarah.

The Lord also assured Abraham regarding Ishmael, saying:

And as for Ishmael, I have heard thee: Behold, I have blessed him, and will make him fruitful, and will multiply him exceedingly; twelve princes shall he beget, and I will make him a great nation.

But my covenant will I establish with Isaac, which Sarah shall bear unto thee at this set time in the next year. (Gen. 17:20-21)

Both Abraham and Sarah were now advanced in years, and it was hard for them to believe that Sarah would have a son. But she did, and he was named Isaac.

The birth of Isaac caused trouble in Abraham's household. Sarah, who herself had suggested his second marriage and had chosen his second wife, now did not want to see Hagar or her son around the camp.

> Wherefore she said unto Abraham, Cast out this bond-woman and her son: for the son of this bondwoman shall not be heir with my son, even with Isaac.
>
> And the thing was very grievous in Abraham's sight because of his son.
>
> And God said unto Abraham, Let it not be grievous in thy sight because of the lad, and because of thy bond-woman; in all that Sarah hath said unto thee, hearken unto her voice; for in Isaac shall thy seed be called.
>
> And also of the son of the bondwoman will I make a nation, because he is thy seed. (Gen. 21:10-13)

Hagar's son married an Egyptian girl. But Isaac, in accordance with his father's wishes, married Rebekah, daughter of Bethuel, son of Nahor, Abraham's brother.

Sarah died at the age of one hundred and twenty-seven. She was buried in the cave of Macphelah, located in a field at Hebron which Abraham purchased from one Ephron, the son of Zohar, for four hundred shekels of silver. This field is the only plot of land which he ever owned. Abraham was a nomad and, like all nomads, roamed over the countryside in search of greener pastures. He had no need to own land. He needed only permission to set up camp temporarily and to graze his flocks.

Although Abraham was very old when Sarah died, he married again.

> Then again Abraham took a wife, and her name was Keturah.

114

And she bare him Zimran, and Jokshan, and Medan, and Midian, and Ishbak, and Shuah.

And Jokshan begat Sheba, and Dedan. And the sons of Dedan were Asshurim, and Letushim, and Leummim.

And the sons of Midian; Ephah, and Epher, and Hanoch, and Abidah, and Eldaah. All these were the children of Keturah.

And Abraham gave all that he had unto Isaac.

But unto the sons of the concubines, which Abraham had, Abraham gave gifts, and sent them away from Isaac his son, while he yet lived, eastward, unto the east country.

And these are the days of the years of Abraham's life which he lived, a hundred three-score and fifteen years.

Then Abraham gave up the ghost, and died in a good old age, an old man, and full of years; and was gathered to his people.

And his sons Isaac and Ishmael buried him in the cave of Macphelah, in the field of Ephron the son of Zohar the Hittite, which is before Mamre. (Gen. 25:1-9)

Today there is a great Islamic mosque over the graves which is called "Al Khalili Mosque" in reference to Abraham, who is called *Abraham Al Khalil*, which means the friend (of God).

Ishmael, Abraham's oldest son, had twelve sons.

And these are the names of the sons of Ishmael, by their names, according to their generations: the firstborn of Ishmael, Nebajoth; and Kedar, and Adbeel, and Mibsam,

And Mishma, and Dumah, and Massa,

Hadar, and Tema, Jetur, Naphish, and Kedemah:

These are the sons of Ishmael, and these are their names, by their towns, and by their castles; twelve princes according to their nations. (Gen. 25:13-16)

115

So Ishmael was the father of twelve tribes, each headed by a prince.

Isaac had only two sons. They were twins. Before they were born, his wife, Rebekah, was told, "Two nations are in thy womb, and two manner of people shall be separated from thy bowels; and the one people shall be stronger than the other people; and the older shall serve the younger."

The first of the twins to be born was a hairy child. He was named Esau, and he became a hunter. His brother was named Jacob. The Bible says that "Jacob was a plain man, dwelling in tents," and that Isaac loved Esau because he often brought him venison, but that Rebekah favored Jacob.

One day Esau returned from one of his hunting trips very hungry. He found Jacob eating "red pottage" made of lentils and asked for some. Jacob demanded Esau's birthright as the first-born in exchange for a bowl of this pottage, a rather high price. But Esau, evidently too hungry to care much about anything, agreed and so lost his right to be the head of the family upon his father's death.

This is not all that he lost to Jacob. Genesis 27 says that shortly before his death Isaac asked Esau to get some venison and make him "savoury meat" to eat, after which he would bestow his last blessing upon him. Rebekah overheard this and as soon as Esau left she insructed Jacob to kill two kids to make "savoury meat" for Isaac and obtain his blessing. When Jacob expressed fear of discovery because "Esau my brother is a hairy man, and I am a smooth man," she put pieces of the kidskin on his arms and neck. Since Isaac was now blind, the trick worked, and Jacob was given the blessing intended for Esau, the firstborn.

When shortly thereafter Esau returned home, cooked his venison, and offered it to his father, the latter was greatly surprised and told Esau, "Thy brother came with subtilty, and hath taken away thy blessing."

Isaac's blessing to Jacob was as follows:

116

God give thee of the dew of heaven, and the fatness of the earth, and plenty of corn and wine:

Let people serve thee, and nations bow down to thee: be lord over thy brethren, and let thy mother's sons bow down to thee: cursed be everyone that curseth thee, and blessed be he that blesseth thee. (Gen. 27:28-29)

This made Jacob master over Esau as well as over other peoples and nations. For some unstated reason, Isaac did not revoke the blessing obtained by Jacob fraudulently. But he blessed Esau thus:

Behold, thy dwelling shall be the fatness of the earth, and of the dew of heaven from above;

And by thy sword shalt thou live, and shalt serve thy brother; and it shall come to pass when thou shalt have the dominion, that thou shalt break his yoke from off thy neck. (Gen. 27:39-40)

This made Esau's subordination to Jacob temporary, for he was assured that the time would come when he would have "the dominion" and "break his yoke."

It seems that there was another drought in the area where Isaac lived, and he thought of going to Egypt. But the Lord told him, "Sojourn in this land, and I will be with thee, and will bless thee; for unto thee, and unto thy seed, I will give all these countries, and I will perform the oath which I sware unto Abraham thy father" (Gen. 26:3).

So Isaac gave up the idea of going to Egypt and settled in Gerar under the protection of Abimelech, king of the Philistines, who inhabited the coastal area of the country, which later was named after them. Here he prospered and his flocks increased, creating a problem of pasture and water. So Abimelech asked him to leave. Isaac had no choice but to go.

But he did not go far, for he "pitched his tent in the valley of Gerar, and dwelt there."

Jacob was sent by his mother to her relatives in Haran, Syria, to escape the wrath of Esau, who threatened to kill him. Another reason for his migration was to marry one of his cousins, for his mother did not want him to marry a Canaanite woman. He married two sisters, Leah and Rachel, the daughters of Laban, Rebekah's brother, after tending Laban's flocks for fourteen years. He worked for Laban six more years, during which he amassed a considerable fortune in livestock.

The first night on the way to Haran, Jacob had a dream in which he saw "a ladder set up on the earth, and the top of it reached to heaven; and behold the angels of God ascending and descending on it," and God was standing at the top of the ladder. Then God spoke to him saying, "the land whereon thou liest, to thee will I give it, and to thy seed" (Gen. 28:13).

Leah gave birth to Reuben, Simeon, Levi, and Judah. Even before their marriage, Jacob loved Rachel more than Leah. But Rachel, seeing that her sister had given him four sons while she had none, feared that his love might wane. So she said to him, "Behold my maid Bilhah, go in unto her; and she shall bear upon my knees, that I may also have children by her" (Gen. 30:3).

He did, and Bilhah in due time gave birth to Dan and Naphtali.

Leah, after giving birth to four sons, stopped bearing children. So she decided to copy her sister and have children by proxy, so to speak, and "took Zilpah, her maid, and gave her Jacob to wife." Zilpah gave birth to Gad and Asher.

A little later Leah gave birth to two sons, Issacher and Zebulon, and to a daughter who was named Dinah. Rachel, after all these years, gave birth to a son, Joseph.

Some difficulties arose between Jacob and his in-laws, and the Lord told him, "Return unto the land of thy fathers, and to thy kindred; and I will be with thee." (But Jacob's father and grandfather owned no land.)

118

So Jacob, in the absence of Laban, who had gone to shear his sheep, put his wives and children on camels, got his flocks and shepherds together and "stole away unawares to Laban the Syrian, in that he told him not that he fled" (Gen. 31:20).

Upon approaching the old camping grounds of his fathers in Palestine, he sent messengers to Esau, who had become a powerful prince and was now called "Edom," to ask forgiveness and also permission to enter "the country of Edom." The messengers returned and told Jacob that Esau had forgiven him and is coming to meet him at the head of four hundred men. This latter statement frightened Jacob, and he prepared for battle. But his fear was groundless. Esau had really come to welcome him and to assure him that he was going to let by-gones be by-gones. And when Esau saw him, he "ran to meet him, and embraced him, and fell on his neck, and kissed him: and they wept" (Gen. 33:4).

Esau and his men returned home to Seir, and Jacob and his entourage followed slowly.

Just before meeting Esau, Jacob is told by God that his name shall be "Israel."

Moving by stages, Jacob, or Israel, came to Shalem, or Salem, (Jerusalem) "and pitched his tent before the city." Here he purchased part of the field in which he camped "for a hundred pieces of money" and erected an altar for "the God of Israel."

God again appeared to Jacob and once more blessed him and said, "And the land which I gave Abraham and Isaac, to thee I will give it, and to thy seed after thee will I give the land."

While they were traveling, Rachel gave birth to another son, and he was named Benjamin. She died in childbirth. So Jacob, like Ishmael, now had twelve sons, and they became the fathers of "the twelve tribes of Israel." Six of the twelve were Leah's children, two were Rachel's, and the remaining four were the children of the two maids.

Esau married two Canaanite girls, one named Adah and the other Aholikamah. He also married Bashemath, his uncle

119

Ishmael's daughter. He had five sons and a dozen grandsons who bore the title of "duke."

XIX

The Fulfillment

It will be observed from the foregoing that Abraham was assured by God that he personally would be given the "land of Canaan," yet he lived and died a nomad, neither ruling over nor owning any part of the country except the burial plot at Hebron. Likewise, the promises made to his son Isaac, and to his grandson Jacob, or Israel, were never fulfilled. Both lived in the country as nomads at the sufferance of the Canaanite or Philistine people and their rulers. Both were buried in the same plot that Abraham had purchased for the purpose of burying his wife Sarah.

The only other land owned by any of them was the small plot that Jacob purchased for the purpose of erecting an altar and which was abandoned when he and his sons moved to Egypt.

It will be recalled that while Jacob was in Syria where he went to escape his brother Esau's wrath, the Lord said to him, "Return unto the land of thy fathers."

Yet his "fathers" Isaac and Abraham owned no land whatsoever, other than the grave site at Hebron. Of course the Lord knew that. Why then did he tell Jacob to go to the land of his fathers?

Abraham had obtained permission from the Canaanites to

live and graze his flocks in their country. Isaac exercised that privilege after his father's death. Could the Lord have meant to tell Jacob to leave Syria and take the flocks he had acquired there to Canaan where he, too, would enjoy the privilege of camping and grazing his flocks as his father and his grandfather had done? Could this have been what God meant when he told these patriarchs that he would give them the land inhabited by the Canaanites?

If this is what God meant, then his promises were fulfilled. But if he meant to give them exclusive possession and control, then obviously he did not fulfill his promises either to the three patriarchs themselves or to their immediate descendants, for Jacob and his sons moved to Egypt, and their descendants remained there four hundred years until Moses led them out.

The reader is familiar with the beautiful story of Joseph, who was sold by his brothers to the Ishmaelite merchants, who took him to Egypt where he became an adviser to the pharaoh, or prime minister, after interpreting a dream for the pharaoh. The Bible says that Joseph later brought his brothers and his father to Egypt and settled them in "the land of Goshen," a lush area in the Nile delta.

Jacob soon died and his sons took him to Palestine and buried him in the cave of Macphelah with his father and grandfather.

It may be relevant to repeat here that before Jacob returned from Syria, his brother Esau had become a powerful chief and Jacob did not dare cross the border without his permission. Esau settled in Seir, the southeastern part of Palestine (the Negeb), permanently and eventually became master of that region. When the children of Israel came out of Egypt under Moses, the children of Esau, or Edom as he was also known, denied them permission to pass through their territory. During the Roman period, Edomite kings ruled in Judea.

These facts indicate that the Lord granted possession of this land or a part of it to Esau, in fulfillment of his promises to Abraham and Isaac. It should be recalled that Esau was the elder son of Isaac, and under the traditional rules of that era, he was supposed to take his father's place upon the latter's death, but hunger caused him to sell that right to Jacob for "a mess of pottage."

This is the interpretation made by Moses, for when he brought the Hebrews out of Egypt, he ordered them not to trespass upon the land of Edom. And Moses' successor, Joshua, did not try to occupy Edom.

The Edomites were never evicted from the land occupied by them. Many of them are still there. They are now known as "Arabs."

The children of Ishmael, Abraham's firstborn, multiplied rapidly in Palestine, with the result that a large number of them, perhaps a majority, emigrated eastward and established themselves in Arabia. Ishmael and his mother, Hagar, are buried in the Sacred Mosque at Mecca alongside the Ka'bah wall. The Ishmaelites, too, were never evicted from this territory. Many of them joined the army of Islam, which conquered and for centuries ruled an empire stretching from Spain to India.

Some Ishmaelite families came with the victorious armies of Islam and settled in Palestine when the country was taken from its Byzantine rulers.

The Bible says that Ishmael, who had twelve sons, "twelve chiefs of as many tribes," settled first in "the wilderness of Paran" but that his descendants moved further east to Arabia. Genesis 25:18 of the Jerusalem Bible says, "He lived in the territory stretching from Havila to Shur, which is to the east of Egypt, on the way to Assyria. He set himself to defy his brothers."

Lot's descendents, the Ammonites and the Moabites, also had permanently settled in the region east of the Jordan River and became the rulers of the territories they occupied long before the sons of Jacob came out of Egypt. Indeed, the Hebrews had to fight Moab to pass through to the Jordan River.

The descendants of Jacob multiplied in Goshen. As time passed, they ceased to think about the land of Canaan. They occupied a rich territory and lived a tranquil life in it. They even forgot the Lord, the God of their forefathers, and learned to worship the local gods.

But history does not stand still. A nationalist revolution drove out the so-called shepherd kings, which ruled the country, and xenophobia raised its head throughout the land.

The Bible says that the new rulers of Egypt drafted the Hebrews (as the Israelites were known) into labor battalions organized to make bricks for Pharaoh's new cities. Evidently some of the Egyptian foremen treated the Hebrew laborers harshly.

The reader will recall the romantic story of Moses, who was rescued from the Nile River by Pharaoh's daughter and was reared to manhood in the royal palace.

One day, while visiting one of the brickworks, Moses saw an Egyptian taskmaster strike a Hebrew laborer. Incensed at the abuse of one of his people, and thinking that no one was looking, he killed the Egyptian. The next day, however, he learned that there was at least one witness to the crime—a Hebrew with whom he had had an argument. Fearing punishment, he at once left Egypt and crossed into "the land of Midian." (Midian was one of Abraham's sons by his third wife Keturah.)

In Midian, Moses became a shepherd for Jethro, the local priest, and married his master's daughter, Zipporah.

One day, while tending Jethro's sheep out in the hills, Moses saw a bush burning but not being consumed by the fire. As he approached to investigate, God spoke to him and told him that He was the God of his fathers and that He wanted him to go back to Egypt and bring the children of Israel out and settle them in "a land flowing with milk and honey," the land He had promised to their ancestors.

Moses, having been brought up in the house of Pharaoh, was taught the religion of the Pharaoh. In his father-in-law's household, he learned about the local religion, which was monotheistic. Like the rest of his kinsmen, he did not know the God of his ancestors. So he said to the Lord, "If I tell the people that the God of their fathers sent me and they ask 'What is his name? what shall I say unto them?' "

Moses returned to Egypt and, as directed, took his brother Aaron to be his spokesman (Moses stuttered) and went to Pharaoh, where he made the historical demand, "Let my people go."

After inflicting ten plagues upon the Egyptians, Moses was finally permitted to lead the Israelites out of Egypt. According to Exodus 12, they numbered "about six hundred thousand on foot that were men, beside children, and a mixed multitude went up also with them; and flocks, and herds, even very much cattle." This exodus of the Hebrews was 430 years after the arrival of Jacob and his sons in the Nile country.

Afraid to follow the direct and well-traveled coastal highway because of the presence of the powerful Philistines along this route, Moses attempted to enter Canaan to the east of the Philistines through the land of Edom, Israel's brother. But Edom denied his request. Later Moses recalled that God had told him regarding the Edomites: " 'Take care not to provoke them. For I will give you none of their land, no, not so much as a foot length of it. I have given the highlands of Seir to Esau as his domain' " (Deut. 2:2-4, The Jerusalem Bible). God also gave Moses similar instructions concerning Moab and Ammon, the descendants of Lot, Abraham's nephew: " 'You are now about to cross Ar, the land of Moab, and to approach the frontier of Ammon. Make no attack on them, and do not provoke them, for I will give you none of the land belonging to the sons of Ammon. I have given it to the sons of Lot as their domain' " (Deut. 2:15-19, The Jerusalem Bible).

Moses obeyed God's instructions.

So they wandered in the desert for forty years, until a new generation was born. Moses himself was denied entry into Canaan because he and his brother Aaron doubted God's ability to provide for their people, despite the numerous miracles that had been performed for them. Both died before the Hebrews entered Palestine.

On the way to the Promised Land, the sons of Israel attacked some of the tribes that denied them passage. Midian, the people who had received and sheltered Moses when he ran away from the Egyptian police, was one of these tribes. The Israelites not only wiped out the Midianite army but also "put every male to death...[and] took the Midianite women captive." Taking the Midianite women captive enraged Moses, for these women, like their Moabite sisters, had led the Hebrew men away from the worship of God. So the women, too, were killed, but the fighting men were permitted to keep the young "virgins."

Sihon, king of Heshbon, and Og, king of Bashan, two Amonrite rulers, also were defeated and their land and all their possessions taken by the Hebrews.

The tribes of Reuben and Gad asked Moses to let them settle in this conquered territory, which was east of the Jordan River. Moses agreed after securing their promise to help the other tribes conquer Canaan. So these two tribes and half of the tribe of Manasseh (one of Joseph's two sons) settled in that area.

Just before his death, Moses had Joshua, the son of Nun, proclaimed commander of the Israelites, and to him was entrusted the task of leading them across the Jordan River to capture Canaan.

Joshua eventually led a new generation of Israelites across Jordan, and after numerous battles with the Canaanites, they conquered the eastern or hilly part of Palestine from the border of Edom in the south to the Lebanese or Phoenician border in the north. This conquered territory comprises the areas later known as Judea and Samaria, and was described as extending "from Dan to Beersheba."

Like Moses before him, Joshua avoided confrontation with the Philistines who dwelt along the Mediterranean coast south of Mount Carmel. He did not consider this area as part of the Promised Land. For in enumerating the tribes or clans that the Hebrews were to dispossess, God never included the Philistines, whose name the country was later to bear. (The Arabs call it *Philistine*—not *Palestine*.)

Indeed, after Joshua had subjugated Canaan, the Philistines, who had "chariots of iron," a weapon that the Hebrews did not possess then, came up, defeated them, and levied tribute upon them.

While the books of Genesis and Exodus do not include the Philistines in the list of nations or tribes to be dispossessed, Genesis 15 says that God promised Abraham's descendants all the land between the Nile and the Euphrates rivers, and Joshua 1:4 says the Promised Land extended from Lebanon and the Euphrates river to the great sea in the west.

These passages raise a serious question concerning the size or extent of the territory promised the patriarchs and contradict the specific orders given by God when the Hebrews under Moses and later under Joshua marched out of Egypt to claim the "Promised Land." It will be recalled that God told Moses not to try to go through the land of the Philistines because that could mean war in which he would lose. And God specifically forbade Israel to try to take any part of Edom's territory or that of Moab and Ammon.

Indeed, if God did really intend to give the Hebrews any part of Egypt, why did he take them out of that country?

The Hebrews were in Egypt when Moses came to lead them into the Promised Land. Had God meant to give them the Egyptian territory east of the Nile River, it would have been much easier to claim it and defend it right then and there while they were in it. Surely the Lord, who inflicted ten plagues on Egypt, parted the waters of the Red Sea to allow the Hebrews to escape, and then drowned the Egyptian army, could have helped the Hebrews to take and to defend the Egyptian territory that he meant them to have. Since the country had been weakened by the plagues inflicted upon it, and its army had been destroyed in the Red Sea, holding a part of it then would have been a cinch.

Likewise, if the Israelites were destined to occupy or colonize any part of Syria, why did not Moses or Joshua try to occupy that territory when they were on its fringes and before crossing the Jordan River? Both leaders, it will be recalled, told the Israelites that their Promised Land was "across Jordan" or west of it, but not east of it. Reuben and Gad had to ask for special dispensation to stay east of the Jordan. They renounced or gave up their share in Canaan, preferring to stay on the east side of the river.

Be that as it may, suffice it to say that the Isrealites did not attempt to go back to Egypt after Moses took them out of it, except as individual immigrants. On the contrary, Egypt, which ruled Jerusalem before the time of Moses, returned again after Solomon's death to exact tribute from its Jewish kings.

Two and a half of the Israelite tribes did settle in Trans-Jordan, but Syria proper and Iraq were never settled by the sons of Jacob. True, David defeated the king of Damascus and exacted tribute from him. But the Hebrews did not annex or colonize his territory. Nor did their armies ever reach the Euphrates.

However, the Assyrians, whose capital, Nineveh, was on the banks of the Euphrates, removed the people of "Israel," the northern kingdom of the Hebrews, to their country, and these ten tribes became assimilated there and were lost as Isrealites. Their blood was mingled with that of the Aramaeans of the country, and they ceased to be a separate people. They are part of the country's "Arab" population of today.

Apparently, no one during the long history of the Hebrews, or the Jews, took these expansionist statements seriously. (There is a political party in Israel today, the Likud, which dreams of the conquest of the entire area between the Nile and the Euphrates.) And when Joshua had completed the conquest of Canaan—"from Dan to Beersheba"—God told him to go ahead and divide this territory among the nine and a half tribes, thus indicating that the job of conquering the Promised Land had been completed. Joshua accepted this conclusion and divided the territory as directed.

The tribe of Judah, of which the "Jews" of today claim to be descended, (the Jews of today are not racially pure. There are too many converts among them.) and Benjamin, the small tribe that eventually merged with Judah, were allotted the area from Jerusalem southward to the border of Edom. The city of Jerusalem itself was not given to them because Joshua was not able to take it. However, it was later taken by David and made part of Judah's territory.

When the division of the conquered territory was completed Joshua said, "And the Lord gave unto Israel all the land which he sware to give unto their fathers; and they possessed it, and dwelt therein" (Josh. 21:43).

In his farewell address to the people, Joshua recited the many favors bestowed on them and quoted God as saying, "And I have given you a land for which ye did not labour, and cities which ye built not, and ye dwell in them; of the vineyards and oliveyards which ye planted not do ye eat" (Josh. 24:13).

This settles the argument concerning the extent or boundaries of the territory promised to Abraham and his descendants. It was the area that Joshua conquered and that comprised only the eastern part of Palestine, from Dan, on the Lebanese border in the north, to Beersheba on the border of Edom in the south. It included neither the land of the Philistines on the coast of the Mediterranean Sea nor the land of Edom. This is what God said, and Joshua and all the Israelites agreed.

The Hebrews were ruthless in war. The inhabitants of several cities were completely exterminated. (See Josh. 10: 26-40.) Once when five kings united their forces against Joshua's army and the latter gained the upper hand with the aid of a terrific hailstorm over the enemy's camp, Joshua stopped the moon and the sun in the sky to gain time to finish off the fleeing enemy.

Despite God's specific orders to kill or drive out the

Canaanites, when Joshua considered his campaign finished and divided the conquered territory among the tribes, numerous Canaanite pockets were still holding out. Although the army of Adoni-Zedek, king of the Jebusites at Jerusalem, was routed, the Jebusites continued to hold out in the fortified city of Jerusalem for several generations. (See Josh. 15:63.) The same situation existed at Gezer and other cities. (See Josh. 16:10; 17:12.)

Some cities whose inhabitants chose not to resist were spared, but their populations were made "hewers of wood and drawers of water" (Josh. 9:21).

No attempt was made by Joshua and his tribal armies to take the coastal plains inhabited by the Philistines. The Bible says: "But Judah did not take Gaza with its territory or Ashkalon with its territory or Ekron with its territory; they could not drive out the inhabitants of the plain, because they had iron chariots. Yahweh was with Judah, and Judah subdued the highlands. (Judg. 1:19, the Jerusalem Bible. The King James version uses a slightly different and seemingly inconsistent wording.)

For a long time after the death of Joshua, the Hebrews had no peace. After they had conquered Canaan, their neighbors, the Philistines, sent an army that crushed the Israelites, disarmed them, and closed up every blacksmith shop in the country, "lest the Hebrews make them swords or spears," making it necessary for the Isrealites to go "down to the Philistines, to sharpen each man his share, and his coulter, and his axe, and his mattock" (I Sam. 13:19-20).

David, who became king of the Israelites c. 990 B.C., changed this situation. He defeated the Philistines and also crushed Edom, Ammon and Moab, the kinfolk of the Israelites, and exacted tribute from Damascus.

XX

The Glory and the Decline of the Israelites

When David's son Solomon ascended the great throne of his father, the Israelites were at the pinnacle of the ladder of success. They had internal unity and prosperity, and the neighbors that had distressed them or disturbed their peace had been subdued and were paying tribute. Solomon became widely recognized as a great king of a great people. He built up the city of Jerusalem which his father had conquered and made it a great and prosperous capital. Here, with the aid of Hiram, king of Tyre, he built the first temple to God, as well as a magnificent palace for himself.

Indeed, this king of the Israelites, the "shepherd" people who had been so despised by the Egyptians that they would not sit at the table with them, married—among many others— a daughter of Pharaoh Psou-sen-nes. And when the city of Gezer rebelled against his rule, his father-in-law sent up an Egyptian army that took the city and gave it to his daughter as a gift.

This golden period in Israel's history lasted only during the reign of David and his son Solomon—about eighty years. (Many scholars say sixty.)

Rivalry had existed between the tribe of Judah and the rest of Israel prior to this period. For years prior to the time of

David, the Bible refers to the Hebrews as "Judah and Israel," thus indicating that Judah for some unstated reason regarded itself as a separate and distinct people. Soon it became not only a separate people from Israel but also its enemy.

David, a member of the tribe of Judah, was first made king over his own tribe only, but later the other tribes submitted to his rule. Following the death of his son Solomon, the tribes in the north and in Trans-Jordan rebelled and refused to recognize Solomon's son Rehoboan as their king. They crowned one Jeroboam as king and made Shechem, and later Samaria, their capital.

This left the king of Jerusalem with only his tribe, Judah, and the remnants of the tribe of Benjamin, which was assimilated by Judah. Judea, as this southern Hebrew kingdom became known, extended from a few miles north of Jerusalem to the border of Edom in the south, and from the Jordan in the east to the Philistine border in the west, barely twenty miles wide and forty miles long. It comprised little more than the southern third of the area now being referred to as the "West Bank." This is an important fact to remember.

To make matters worse for Solomon's son, a new pharaoh of Egypt, Shishak, sent an army across Sinai and made him a tributary of Egypt.

Jerusalem not only ceased to be the political capital of all the Hebrews but also ceased to be their spiritual center, for Jeroboam, the king of "Israel," as the northern kingdom was called, built sanctuaries for his people within his borders and thus made it unnecessary for them to go to Solomon's temple at Jerusalem to worship. Having lost its independence, Jerusalem also lost much of its importance as the spiritual center of the Hebrews.

The northern kingdom, too, was made a tributary of a more powerful neighbor. Assyria, then Egypt's rival, first made Israel a tributary but in 722 B.C. wiped it out completely. The majority of the Israelites were taken into Assyria. They were replaced by Arameans and Bedouins from Syria. These became integrated with the Israeli remnants in the country and formed the people who became known as "Samaritans," in reference to their capital, Samaria. These Samaritans were so despised by the Jews that they would not have any intercourse with them. The reader will recall the story of Jesus and the Samaritan woman at the well recorded in John 4:7-26.

The Israelites who were taken to Assyria soon became completely integrated with their neighbors and lost their identity as Israelites. They became known in history books as "the lost ten tribes of Israel."

In 586 B.C., a revitalized Babylonia sent an army into Palestine, destroyed Jerusalem, (including Solomon's temple) and took the cream of Judah as prisoners into Babylonia. Thus ended Israelite and Jewish rule in Palestine.

Seventy years after the destruction of Jerusalem by Babylon, the Persians, after conquering the Babylonian empire, gave the Jews permission to go back to Judea. Ezra 2:64-67 says that 42,360 Jews returned and rebuilt Jerusalem. But they did not become an indepentent nation. Judea and all Palestine simply became a Persian, instead of a Babylonian, vassal. The country merely changed masters and continued to be ruled by a foreign governor.

And when Alexander the Great defeated the Persians, Palestine, including Judea, became part of the Greek empire.

About the middle of the second century B.C., an attempt to suppress Judaism by Antiochus IV caused a Jewish uprising that was led by a priest named Mattathias and his son Maccabaeus. Not only did these rebels reestablish Jewish worship at the temple of Jerusalem but they also overran Edom, the Philistine coastal cities, and Galilee and imposed the religion of Judah upon the conquered people.

But soon the Roman legions came and occupied Jerusalem and all of Palestine.

A Jewish rebellion caused the Romans to destroy most of Jerusalem. In A.D. 70, a second uprising resulted in the complete wiping out of the city. A new city, built on the site later and called Aelia Capitolina, was declared out of bounds for Jews.

In A.D. 637, the Moslem Arabs occupied Palestine and, of course, Aelia Capitolina, or Jerusalem, as it was again called, and which had become a center of pilgrimage by Christians after the conversion of the Emperor Constantine to Christianity in the fourth century A.D.

Palestine, like Syria and Iraq, soon was Arabized. Arabic replaced Aramaic and Greek, and Islam became the dominant religion.

The European crusaders occupied Palestine and in A.D. 1099 established a "Latin kingdom" under a European prince. Although periodically reenforced by fresh troops from home, they were finally defeated, and Arab sovereignty was restored over the region in 1187.

Arab sovereignty was ended in 1516 when the Turks wrested the Khalifate from the Arabs. However, Palestine remained an Arab country in population, language, and culture, and it enjoyed peace and security as part of the great Ottoman Empire.

In 1918 a British army, assisted by the Arabs, drove the Turks out of the country. The British then opened its gates to Jewish immigration, despite the objections of the Arabs. In May 1948, the newly arrived Jewish immigrants, now numbering 650,000, drove 80 percent of the Palestinian Arabs out and proclaimed the establishment of the state of "Israel" in 80 percent of the country but not in Judea or Samaria. These remained Arab.

XXI

Recapitulations

1. The "promise" was originally made to Abraham and his "seed" before any children were born to him. God specifically assured Abraham that He would make a nation of Ishmael "because he is thy seed." (Gen. 21:13).

History records that when the Muslim Arab army took Damascus from the Romans and prepared to move on to Palestine, its commander, Khalid ibn-al-Walid, sent a message to the Roman commander in Palestine saying: "God promised to give the country to Abraham and his descendants. We are the children of Abraham and have come to take possession of our sacred heritage. So please take your troops and go in peace."

But the Roman commander, who was, like all Romans of the time, Christian, did not take the Muslim commander's advice, and a battle followed, which ended in the triumph of Islam.

This was seven centuries after the Jews had left or had been expelled from Palestine.

Khalid ibn-al-Walid's argument is not so farfetched. The children of Ishmael, Abraham's firstborn, were entitled to inherit from their grandfather equally with those of Isaac. The fact that Ishmael's mother was a maid did not make any difference. Four of Jacob's twelve sons were the children of maids. But that fact did not bar them from inheriting equally with their brothers. When Sarah suggested to her husband that he "go in" unto Hagar, it was for the specific purpose of having an heir.

True, Sarah changed her mind later and ordered Hagar and her son out of the camp, but there is nothing to show that God did. On the contrary, he sent his angel to reassure Hagar concerning her child's future. The Bible also shows that the children of Ishmael multiplied and progressed faster than those of Isaac.

Likewise, the descendants of Esau must be included among Abraham's heirs. They were allotted the southeastern part of Palestine, the Negeb.

2. The Bible contains conflicting statements concerning the size of the "promised" land. At one time Abraham was told by God that he would get "all the land which thou seest," which would be a very small part of the country. At another time the future gift was enlarged to include the entire region between "the river of Egypt unto the great river, the river Euphrates." In an even more generous moment God is reported to have said, "Everywhere thy feet trod that shall be yours." (This would include Russia, Europe, and the United States.) This conflict, however, was settled when Joshua finished his conquests, which included only the eastern part of Palestine, extending "from Dan to Beersheba," and then wrote, "And the Lord gave unto Israel all thè land which he sware to give unto their fathers." The Israelites accepted this and settled down to enjoy the fruits of their conquests.

3. When Joshua, in obedience to God's orders, partitioned the promised and now conquered land, he gave the tribe of Judah the area west of the Dead Sea extending from Jerusalem to Hebron. But Jerusalem itself was not included in Judah's territory then because it had not been conquered.

4. The Israelite tribes split into two often warring kingdoms. Judah and Benjamin formed one kingdom with Jerusalem as its capital. Their territory became known as "Judea," and they began to be known as "Jews." The other tribes

formed the northern kingdom and made Samaria their capital. They retained the name "Israel."

5. Although the "land of Canaan" was occupied and colonized by the Hebrews, they never were the sole occupants of it. Many Canaanite pockets remained in it, including the entire population of some cities.

The Edomites and the Philistines who inhabited the southern part of Palestine were not dispossessed by the Hebrews. Their descendants as well as the descendants of the Canaanites who were not killed off are still there and are fighting the new Israel. But they all are called "Arabs."

6. In 722 B.C. the northern kingdom, Israel, was completely wiped out, and most of its people were carried to Assyria, where they became totally assimilated with the Assyrians. Their former land in Palestine was repopulated by people from Syria, who mingled with the remnant of the Israelites and Canaanites and became known as "Samaritans." A few Samaritans are still in this area, adhering to their ancient customs and beliefs. The majority, however, like the Canaanites, the Edomites, and the Philistines, as well as thousands of Jews, converted to Christianity and later to Islam and became Arabs in customs and in speech. So no one today can make a claim to Samaria in the name of the lost ten tribes of Israel.

7. Judea outlived Israel. But its turn came in 586 B.C. when Babylon's armies destroyed Jerusalem and the Temple of Solomon and took the leading Jewish families to Babylon.

8. Some 42,000 Jews were allowed by Persia, which overran the Babylonian empire, to return to Judea and to rebuild Jerusalem. But Judea remained a vassal of Persia until Alexander the Great destroyed the Persian empire.

9. The Jews rebelled against the Greeks and for a time succeeded in establishing their rule, only to be crushed by the Romans who destroyed Jerusalem in A.D. 70.

The Arabs came in A.D. 637 and drove the Romans from Palestine, Syria, and Jordan. The area soon became Arab. It was still Arab when the Zionists came in recent years and established the state of Israel by force of arms.

XXII

Conclusions

1. God's promise was made to Abraham and his "seed," meaning his physical, biological descendants. No other persons were included. Although Abraham had many sons, the heirs were somehow narrowed down to Isaac's son Jacob and through him to his twelve sons. When the promised land was conquered five centuries later, it was divided among the descendants of these sons, and Judah (with Benjamin) was allotted the eastern part of Palestine between Jerusalem and Beer Sheba. So those who claim any part of Palestine as "Jews" must show descent from Judah and their claim must be restricted to Judea. Converts to Judaism like the Khazars in Russia or the Chicago black people who emigrated to Israel and were accepted as "Jews," not being Abraham's "seed," have no valid claim. If we admit the claims of these converts to the religion of Judah and Abraham we would open the door to the whole Christian and Islamic worlds because both assert that they are following the faith of Abraham. Indeed, the Christian church calls itself the "New Israel," and the Arabs refer to the ancient patriarch as "Abouna Ibrahim"—Father Abraham—and remember that the Jews themselves have not agreed on who is a Jew.

2. Those who qualify as the descendants of Judah may not

claim the lands in which their enemy, the ten tribes of Israel, lived. The Hebrew tribes were expressly forbidden to transfer land from one tribe to another.

Moses, after consulting God, ruled that land may not be transferred from one tribe to another. He even forbade girls who had inherited land to marry outside their tribe.

And every daughter, that posseseth an inheritance in any tribe of the children of Isreal, shall be wife unto one of the family of the tribe of her father, that the children of Israel may enjoy every man the inheritance of his fathers.

Neither shall the inheritance remove from one tribe to another tribe; but every one of the tribes of the children of Israel shall keep himself to his own inheritance. (Num. 36:8-9)

This and the history of the wars between the kingdoms of Judah and Isreal make it clear that the Jews of today have no rights under God's promise to the northern part of Palestine. "Judea" covered only the area between Ramallah in the north and Beersheba in the south, the Dead Sea in the east and the land of the ancient Philistines in the west.

Moreover, there is a question whether those Jews now in Israel numbering three million out of fourteen million in the world today may expropriate the rights of the Jewish majority, which has no plans to immigrate to Palestine.

3. The Jewish state, established in 1948 and cleverly named "Israel" for propaganda purposes, was established neither in Judea nor even in the area of the northern kingdom, Israel, but mostly on land that had been expressly denied by God to the tribes of Israel. Only a tiny part of Judea, a corridor to the western suburb of Jerusalem, was included in it. The occupation of this corridor, as well as the occupation of the new Jerusalem, was in violation of the U.N. partition resolution.

4. This brings us to a very important question: Did God

promise to give the land of Canaan to the Hebrews to have and to hold unconditionally "forever," as Genesis says?

It seems that the terms "forever" and "everlasting" were used rather loosely. For example, we may cite the Lord's promise to David: "Thy throne shall be established for ever" (II Sam. 7:16). But shortly thereafter, when David arranged the death of Uriah the Hittite in order to marry his widow, the prophet Nathan told him, "Now therefore the sword shall never depart from thine house; because thou hast despised me, and hast taken the wife of Uriah the Hittite to be thy wife" (II Sam. 12:10). David's throne was abolished some 2500 years ago. It would thus seem that the Lord always reserved the right to terminate a blessing that he had bestowed if the recipient subsequently displeased him.

Moses made it definitely clear that continued possession of the land of Canaan depended upon the future conduct of the Israelites. Before they crossed the Jordan River, he told them:

See, I have set before thee this day life and good, and death and evil;

In that I command thee this day to love the Lord thy God, to walk in his ways, and to keep his commandments, and his statutes, and his judgments, that thou mayest live and multiply: and the Lord thy God shall bless thee in the land whither thou goest to possess it.

But if thine heart turn away, so that thou wilt not hear, but shalt be drawn away, and worship other gods, and serve them;

I denounce unto you this day, that ye shall surely perish, and that ye shall not prolong your days upon the land, whither thou passest over Jordan to go to possess it. (Deut. 30:15-18)

Despite the fact that the original promise to the patriarchs was unconditional, we have here a definite condition attached to the gift.

Chapter 26 of Leviticus and chapter 28 of Deuteronomy go into details in reciting the blessings that the Lord proposed to pour upon the Israelites so long as they obeyed his commandments and the severe punishments that would be inflicted upon them if they went astray. This policy of the carrot and the stick was affirmed centuries later by the prophets of Judah. Isaiah 1:19-20 says, "If ye be willing and obedient, ye shall eat the good of the land: But if ye refuse and rebel, ye shall be devoured with the sword: for the mouth of the Lord hath spoken it."

Speaking to Solomon after the temple was built, God said that He had "Hallowed this house,... and mine eyes and mine heart shall be there perpetually." However, he added, "But if ye shall at all turn from following me, ye or your children,... then will I cut off Israel out of the land which I have given them; and this house, which I have hallowed for my name, will I cast out of my sight; and Israel shall be a proverb and a byword among all people"(I Kings 9:6-7).

Apparently the Israelites did not continue to observe God's commandments, and for that reason the Lord first sent the Assyrians who wiped Israel off the map for good, and later he sent the Babylonians who destroyed the kingdom of Judah.

> But they mocked the messengers of God, and despised his words, and misused his prophets, until the wrath of the Lord arose against his people, till there was no remedy.
>
> Therefore he brought upon them the king of the Chaldees, who slew their young men with the sword. (II Chron. 36:16-17)

Whether this severe punishment was deserved is besides the point. It is not for us to say whether the judgments of the Lord are fair. We do not know, for example, whether the Canaanites were so bad that they deserved the punishment inflicted upon them by the Israelites. As far as the Bible reveals, they were friendly and hospitable to Abraham and to Isaac and Jacob and his sons also. Indeed, Melchizedek, the king of Jerusalem, who also was "the priest of the most high God," blessed Abraham, and the two became friends. Yet God, unbeknown to Melchizedek, promised Abraham the land belonging to this pious monarch's people.

Neither do we understand why God, after ordering Moses to return to Egypt and lead the Israelites out, met him on the road to that country and tried to kill him. "And it came to pass by the way in the inn, that the Lord met him, [Moses] and sought to kill him." (Ex. 4:24.)

5. There is nothing in the Bible that could reasonably be interpreted as predicting the resurrection of the Jewish kingdom, which was destroyed by the Babylonians and the Romans.

Those who believe that the rise of contemporary Israel was foretold by the prophets rely largely on certain passages taken out of context, such as that found in Amos 9:11, 15, which says:

> In that day will I raise up the tabernacle of David that is fallen, and close up the breaches thereof; and I will raise up his ruins, and I will build it as in the days of old. . . .
> And I will plant them upon their land, and they shall no more be pulled up out of their land which I have given them, saith the Lord thy God.

Amos, in the first verse of the first chapter of his book, dates his vision to "the days of Uzziah king of Judah." This places him in the early part of the eighth century B.C. Clearly, therefore, his prophecy refers to the return of the Jews from the Babylonian captivity.

Another Biblical passage often quoted is that found in Isa. 2:3-4:

And many people shall go and say, Come ye, and let us go up to the mountain of the Lord, to the house of the God of Jacob; and he will teach us of his ways, and we will walk in his paths: for out of Zion shall go forth the law, and the word of the Lord from Jerusalem.

And he shall judge among the nations, and shall rebuke many people: and they shall beat their swords into plowshares, and their spears into pruninghooks: nation shall not lift up sword against nation, neither shall they learn war any more.

We cannot see how this prophesy of complete world disarmament and the reign of universal peace can be even remotely related to the Zionist state established in 1948 "by fire and sword" and which continues to live by the sword.

Because modern Israel was created by the sword and by ordinary men, Orthodox Jews have refused to recognize it and are resisting its un-Jewish laws. They believe that Isaiah's prophesy will be fulfilled and peace will reign on earth when the Messiah comes.

Of course, a true Christian will say that Jesus put an end to all speculation concerning the reestablishment of a Jewish state, be it a kingdom, a republic, or a theocracy. He proclaimed a new dispensation—a new covenant—and advised people to forget about the kingdom of Judah and seek the Kingdom of God instead. When asked whether the Jews should continue to pay taxes to the Roman government, he advised the questioner to "render unto Caesar the things which are Caesar's." Translated, this advice simply meant, "Cease thinking of the reestablishment of a Jewish kingdom."

We wonder what the situation of the Jews, and of the world, would be today, had they followed this advice and had not rebelled against Rome.

Jesus rejected the idea of a resurrected Jewish kingdom and the notion of racial exclusiveness (upon which Zionist rulers in

143

Palestine insist) as well as the theory that salvation depended on one's descent or racial origin. He opened the gates of the Kingdom of God to all men, regardless of race or social standing.

> And I say unto you, That many shall come from the east and west, and shall sit down with Abraham, and Isaac, and Jacob, in the kingdom of heaven. (Matt. 8:11)

> For whosoever shall do the will of my Father which is in heaven, the same is my brother, and sister, and mother. (Matt. 12:50)

> My mother and my brethren are these which hear the word of God, and do it. (Luke 8:21)

> There is neither Jew nor Greek there is neither bond nor free, there is neither male nor female: for ye are all one in Christ Jesus.

> And if ye be Christ's then are ye Abraham's seed, and heirs to the promise. (Gal. 3:28-29)

Obviously these teachings do not support the allegation that the establishment of the present Jewish state was preordained by the almighty God or that it represents fulfillment of prophecy.

Finally, it should be borne in mind that the sons of Jacob were destined to "spread abroad" in all directions. We read that the Lord told Jacob, "And thy seed shall be as the dust of the earth; and thou shalt spread abroad to the west, and to the east, and to the north, and to the south: and in thee and in thy seed shall all the families of the earth be blessed" (Gen 28:14).

This indicates that the Diaspora may not have been a punishment inflicted upon the descendants of Jacob but a preordained destiny planned by God for the benefit of the world and that the presence of Jews in different nations is designed to help those nations. And there is no denying the fact that Jews have been in the vanguard of many social and political reform movements in many countries. They have made significant contributions to knowledge in many fields, especially in the fields of mathematics, physics, medicine, and philosophy. These contributions were made not while the Jews were still in Judea but while they were in other countries after their dispersion.

XXIII

The "Homeless Jew" and his "Historic Connection" With Palestine

It has been frequently argued by some misguided Christians—most of whom are motivated more by an inner feeling of antipathy rather than sympathy toward the Jews—that they are a stateless people without a country and should have a homeland and a state of their own. It is also argued that since their ancestors once lived in Palestine, they should be allowed—nay, they have a right—to go to Palestine, and build a Jewish state in it. This latter argument was sold by the Zionists to well-educated diplomats at the Paris Peace Conference and at the League of Nations.

These arguments raise three questions.

1. Are the Jews homeless and stateless?
2. Are all the Jews of today descended from the Jews who lived in Judea two thousand years ago?
3. Is a "connection" that ended two thousand years ago sufficient to support a claim to an inhabited country today?

Is it true that the Jews are a homeless and stateless people? Is our current secretary of state, Dr. Henry A. Kissinger, who has been presiding over the National Security Council since

146

1969, or U.S. Attorney General Edward H. Levi, homeless and stateless? Are the Jewish members of the Congress of the United States and the thousands of Jews in the executive department of our Government really homeless and stateless? Are the thousands of Jewish college professors, lawyers, judges, and physicians in the United States homeless and stateless? Are the thousands of Jews who run most of America's retail trade homeless and stateless?

There are six million Jews in this country, about half the world Jewry. Although most of them sympathize with Israel, I am sure if you asked one of them whether he is homeless or stateless, he would be terribly offended—and justly so. This country is as much his as it is yours or mine. This is true of Jews in other countries. Even in the Soviet Union today, Jews participate in the government and enjoy equality with other races, Zionist claims of anti-Semitism notwithstanding. Jews were members of the inner circle of the group that overthrew the Czar's regime.

Perhaps we should point out here that many prominent Jews in England and in the United States opposed the Zionists' demands for a Jewish state in 1917, insisting that Jews are not stateless or homeless, that they are full citizens of the countries in which they live, and that these countries are home to them. They feared that the demand for a Jewish state would have far-reaching repercussions and might compromise their own status and raise questions concerning their own loyalties to their countries.

In the United States, prominent Jews formed the American Council for Judaism, whose sole mission has been to fight Zionist activity and disassociate American Jewry from Zionism. The membership of this organization within a short period passed the one hundred thousand mark. Its factual and scholarly publications won the respect of the reader whether he was a Jew or a Gentile. They argued that Jews in America were American citizens of the Jewish faith and did not differ from American citizens of the Catholic or the

147

Baptist persuasion. Zionist pressure following the Six Day War, however, discouraged many of their members.

When Ben-Gurion, prime minister of Israel, said that it was the duty of Jews in the Diaspora to aid Israel, some American Jews became incensed and protested vigorously.

It was to quiet this opposition that the following proviso was inserted in the Balfour Declaration: "Nothing shall be done which may prejudice . . . the rights and political status enjoyed by Jews in any other country."[22]

Indeed, opposition to Zionism ante-dates the formation of the Zionist Organization. A meeting of Reform Jewish Rabbis in Pittsburgh in 1885 adopted the following stand:

> We consider ourselves no longer a nation but a religious community. And therefore expect neither a return to Palestine, nor a sacrificial worship under the administration of the sons of Aaron, nor the restoration of any of the laws concerning the Jewish state.[23]

Zionism had little appeal to Jews until Hitler came to its aid. The demand for a state did not surface until 1945.

It may be appropriate here to ask the old question: What is a Jew? Racially the Jews are like Americans, a mixed race. Religiously they are divided, and one sect refuses to recognize the "man-made state" of Israel. The Naturei Karta is waiting for the Messiah to come and reign in Jerusalem. Then there are the thousands of atheists and agnostics who reject the religion of Judah, make fun of the Torah and the idea of the Promised Land, and still are accepted in Israel as "Jews."

We must also bear in mind that Palestine is the birthplace

---

22. The British did not do anything that directly affected the Jews in other countries. But Zionist activities, which put Israel's interests above those of other nations, have called into question the "double loyalty" problem.

23. Rabbi Elmer Berger, *The Jewish Dilemma* (New York: 1945), p. 240.

of Christianity and is sacred to Christians everywhere. It is also sacred to the followers of Islam. It contains the most sacred churches of Christendom and some of Islam's most hallowed mosques. The Jews have no such shrines there today and have had none since the temple originally built by Solomon was finally destroyed by the Romans.

Conceding, for the sake of argument, that the Jews are homeless, in need of a homeland of their own, and that their "historical connection" with Palestine justifies their re-occupation of the country, would that justify driving out its legitimate inhabitants?

XXIV

The Balfour Declaration and the Mandate

As we have seen, the Balfour Declaration was a promise by the British government to help the Zionists establish "a national home for the Jewish people." Britain had no right to make such a promise because Palestine was not British territory. The Balfour Declaration was legally invalid and morally reprehensible. True, this promise was incorporated in the League of Nations mandate, and it may be said, therefore, that it gained international sanction. But the so-called League of Nations was dominated by Great Britain. The United States, Russia, Germany, and the scores of African and Asian countries that have won their independence since that time were not members and did not take part in the distribution of the mandates or in formulating them. The Arab world was occupied by European armies. At any rate, the League, like Britain, had no right to transfer a country from one people to another, and it actually did not do that.

Indeed, the mandate was not prepared by the League of Nations staff. It was drafted in London by the Colonial Office and the Zionist Organization, and then it was submitted to the League for *pro forma* approval.

But let us assume, for the sake of argument, that the mandate was a valid instrument in international law. The fact remains that it authorized the creation of a "national home" for the Jews, not a state. Neither the Balfour Declaration nor the mandate authorized or contemplated the eviction of the Palestinians from their homes and country. Both provided that nothing should be done that might affect their rights.

Article 22 of the League of Nations Covenant said that the mandate system was intended to teach certain newly liberated countries the art of self-government and to lead them toward independence. It further provided:

> Certain communities formerly belonging to the Turkish Empire have reached a stage of development where their existence as independent nations can be provisionally recognized subject to the rendering of administrative advice and assistance by a Mandatory until such time as they are able to stand alone. The wishes of these communities must be a principal consideration in the selection of the Mandatory.

The "communities" referred to here are Iraq, Syria, Lebanon, Jordan, and Palestine. Syria and Lebanon were placed under French mandates and later attained independence. Iraq, Jordan, and Palestine were placed under the British. Iraq has become independent. So has Jordan. Palestine alone, being saddled with the national home, has been denied independence, and a Jewish state has been built in it, in defiance of its people, and in violation of the League's Covenant and of Article 6 of the mandate, which provided:

> The administration of Palestine, while insuring that *the rights and position* of other sections of the population [i.e., the Arabs] are not prejudiced, shall facilitate Jewish immigration under suitable conditions. [italics mine]

Surely the creation of the Jewish state in Palestine and the expulsion of the legitimate inhabitants and owners of the land was not authorized either by the Balfour Declaration or the League of Nations mandate.

XXV

The United Nations Partition Resolution

The 1947 General Assembly's resolution, which is the only instrument having an international character recommending the creation of a Jewish state in Palestine, was torn up by the Jews in Palestine who were backed by the World Zionist Organization, before the ink on it had time to dry.

This resolution, as we have seen, divided Palestine into seven parts and called for the creation of a Jewish state in three of them and an Arab state in three other parts. The seventh part, which comprised Jerusalem and Bethlehem, was to be internationalized for religious considerations. The State of Israel was established not only in the three parts designated for the Jewish state but also in half of the territory reserved for the Arab state as well as a considerable part of Jerusalem.

Moreover, the U.N. resolution required both states to be democratic in character and to give their citizens equal rights in political and civil matters without regard to race or religion. Israel, although touted as "a bastion of democracy in the Middle East," is not a democratic state and has not practiced true democracy within its borders except toward Jews. As we have seen, most of the Arab population was driven out of their homes and country when Israel was established. Those Arabs who escaped expulsion and remained in their homes are regarded as second-class citizens.

The Law of Return, promulgated in 1950, provides in substance that any Jew can come to Israel from any country and can become an Israeli citizen the moment he arrives. But a Christian or a Moslem who was driven out of the country during the fighting that followed the adoption of the Partition Resolution could not return to his town or village in the area that became Israel.

Israel assumed from the beginning the character of a racial theocratic state and did that while Jews everywhere else were and still are fighting racial and religious bigotry.

Since Israel violated the U.N. Partition Resolution by taking more territory than this resolution specified, and by expelling the Arabs and expropriating their property, it cannot now claim legitimacy under that resolution. Indeed, Israel has not only violated or defied U.N. resolutions but has violated and defied the U.N. Charter itself. Her innumerable and continuing military attacks upon her neighbors, for which she has been condemned by the U.N. a number of times, have made her a rebel against the world peace organization and have earned her severe sanctions and even expulsion from it. She has been spared such punishment only by the grace of the United States.

Had Israel adhered to the provisions of the Partition Resolution, had not taken more territory than that resolution specified, and had not expelled the Arabs, she would have ground for claiming legitimacy under it. She cannot claim rights under a U.N. resolution the major and basic provisions of which she has violated and continues to violate in defiance of the United Nations.

XXVI

The Rebel Child

We have seen that the Jewish state is an illegal state established by foreigners who came from many countries and still are coming. This state was established on land that did not belong to them and to which they had no title under any known law, human or divine. Even the name "Israel" belonged to another people. It is a state established by the sword, has lived so far by the sword, and continues to live by the sword.

The sword with which Israel was created and which she wields today is not her own. Moreover, in the beginning this sword was not wielded by her own men. It was a British sword wielded by some forty thousand to one hundred thousand British soldiers from 1918 until 1948, when the Jews in Palestine became strong enough to vanquish the Palestinians.

When fighting erupted in 1948 between the Arabs and the newly proclaimed state of Israel, the U.N. Security Council, in order to keep the war within limits and minimize the loss of life and property, decreed an embargo on the shipment of arms to the combatants. But Israel quickly nullified this embargo by obtaining weapons from Communist bloc nations. It was Israel, not Egypt, that first introduced Communist arms into the region.

Following the signing of the armistice agreements between Israel and the adjoining Arab states in February 1949, the West European nations—with United States encouragement and financing—became the arms suppliers to Israel. Since the 1967 war, the United States took over the supply of arms to Israel openly and in a big way and so kept Israel militarily stronger than all the Arab states around her combined. As we have noted, during the October 1973 war, Secretary of State Henry Kissinger airlifted to Israel over two billion dollars worth of war jets, tanks, missiles, etc., and Congress quickly voted the money as a gift to pay for these highly sophisticated and, in some categories, scarce weapons. And this gift was made while the United States was in a difficult economic situation and the Government was conducting an economy campaign.

As a result of this very generous supply of weapons, Israel, whose population has increased from 650,000 in 1947 to over 3,000,000 in 1975, is still rated by all knowledgeable persons as the strongest military power in the Middle East. Her superiority in arms has been demonstrated in 1948, 1956, 1967, and also in 1973, after American arms began to arrive. Today, after receiving additional quantities of arms from the United States, she is once more challenging the Arabs. Indeed, she is hinting at a preemptive war. The cost of 1973-1974 weapons was over $2,500,000,000. For 1975 she requested $4,000,000,000 worth, half of it to be free of charge —a donation from the American taxpayer.

Israel has defied not only the Arabs—she has continuously defied the United Nations, and often despite America's vote against her. Indeed, Israel has been at war with the United Nations since its birth.

That is true in regard to the repatriation of the Palestinians; it is true in regard to her innumerable and often massive military attacks against neighboring Arab towns and villages in violation of the armistice agreements and the provisions of the United Nations Charter; and it is true in regard to the annexation of the Arab city of Jerusalem and her refusal to evacuate the territories occupied in the 1967 war.

Israel came into being pursuant to a U.N. resolution. But she promptly began to violate this very resolution and ignore the scores of resolutions that followed it. Her attitude toward the world peace organization was frankly expressed by Prime Minister Golda Meir, the former Michigan school teacher who said, "The U.N. passes a resolution not to our liking, so what?"

Israel has ignored U.N. Resolution 194, approved December 11, 1948, and reaffirmed annually since, which provided:

> Resolves that the refugees wishing to return to their homes and live at peace with their neighbors should be permitted to do so at the earliest practicable date, and that compensation should be paid for the property of those choosing not to return and for loss of or damage to property, which, under principles of international law or in equity, should be made good by the governments or the authorities responsible.

She has done this despite the fact that both the United States and the Soviet Union have consistently backed it.

Back in 1949 the Israeli Ministry of Foreign Affairs merely said "The clock cannot be turned back." Yet Zionism turned it back 2500 years to restore Jewish rule. When later the U.N. pressed the question, it was told "Israel is a sovereign state, and . . . must apply its own authority and discretion as to who shall and who shall not enter its territory." To the press at different times she has offered different excuses for her refusal to permit the return of the Palestinians to their homes. One of these was lack of living space. But Zionist leaders in the early days of the Zionist movement often assured the Arabs that Jewish immigration would not hurt them; on the contrary, it would raise their standard of living.

Since Israel was created, two and a half million Jews have

been brought into the country. As the sources of Jewish immigrants began to dry up elsewhere, a campaign was mounted to force the U.S.S.R. to change its emigration laws and allow Jews to emigrate freely to Israel. This campaign has been successful, thanks to the behind-the-scenes efforts of our secretary of state, Henry Kissinger, but it has not been successful enough to suit Israel's manpower needs. So in 1974, the U.S. Congress included in a revised trade and tariff bill a provision denying Russia equal treatment with other nations unless it changes its emigration laws to give the Jews special privileges.

The result of this action—the adoption of the amendment to the trade bill pushed by Sen. Henry Jackson, who has declared his candidacy for the presidency of the United States in 1976 and is counting heavily on Jewish support to send him to the White House[24]—was that the Kremlin, feeling highly insulted by this intrusion into its internal affairs by the Congress of the United States, rejected this bill *in toto* and also abrogated a trade agreement signed in 1972. It also directed its trade elsewhere with the result that unemployment in the United States reached higher levels.

It should be stated here that the United States has been paying the cost of transporting Jews from Russia to Israel, as well as the cost of building homes for them in Palestine.

The State Department in a news release dated October 9, 1973, stated:

Migration of Jews from the U.S.S.R. through Austria to Israel has been continuous for more than 15 years, and principal financial support for the movement has come from the United States. U.S. Government assistance and

---

24. In 1972, Israeli Ambassador Rabin, who is now premier, told American Jews: "If we cannot get Jackson, we will take Nixon." He also told them of Nixon's generosity toward Israel and his political support of the Jewish state.

contributions to Jewish voluntary agencies total hundreds of millions of dollars in cash, commodities, and supplies. Most of the support has gone for resettlement of migrants in Israel. But substantial sums have been spent also in Austria,[25] the country of transit because of its geographic location and its long dedication to principles of humanitarianism and protection of the rights of man.

The United States, instead of using its good offices to induce Israel to allow the repatriation of the Arab refugees, is aiding the settlement of Russian and other foreign Jews on the refugees' lands and thus making their repatriation more difficult.

Incidentally, these new housing units are usually built by the Palestinian Arabs who were reduced to "hewers of wood and drawers of water" as in Joshua's time.

While visiting Jerusalem in 1972, this writer met an American tourist at the Intercontinental Hotel. One morning, as she was reading the *Jerusalem Post,* she saw that the United States Government had given Israel—given, not loaned—$80,000,000 for building houses for Soviet Jews who come to Israel. The lady all but "blew her top." She said she had led a drive in her community to build an apartment house for elderly persons, and asked for a government loan of two million dollars, and was told that the Government did not have the money. "How is it," she demanded, "that they have eighty million dollars to give away for a morally questionable project but don't have two million to loan us so we can take care of our own elderly people?"

I suggested that she ask her Congressman and senators that question. But I doubt that she did.

A second reason given by Israel for not allowing the

---

25. Austria early provided staging and training camps for Soviet Jews going to Israel. But Palestinian pressure forced Chancellor Bruno Kreisky, who is Jewish, to change his policy.

Palestinian refugees to return home is that they would create a problem of security in case of war with the Arab states. But it is an undeniable fact that the Palestinians who remained in the territory that became Israel have been, unlike those in the refugee camps, rather peaceful and docile even during the last three wars. The reason is obvious. They do not wish to be punished or expelled. The refugees, however, have nothing to lose and believe any change is better than living in those miserable camps and subsisting on international charity. So they carry out suicide attacks on the Israelis.

The last explanation offered by the Israelis in and out of the government for refusing to allow the repatriation of the Palestinians is that they want the state to remain Jewish, and the return of the Palestinians would make it binational and they don't want that. This, of course, is the real reason. And it is a valid one if the state must remain Jewish. The Zionists, from the beginning, wanted a totally Jewish state. This is why they expelled the Arabs back in 1948. And that is why they reject the Palestine Liberation Organization's proffered solution of a democratic state in which Moslems, Jews, and Christians would have equal rights. Yet, when the U.N. General Assembly said Zionism is a form of racism they screamed to high heaven.

So we have the ironic situation of Jews everywhere outside Israel fighting for democratic principles and equal rights for all persons irrespective of race or religion while those in Israel refuse to have any but Jews in that state. And to protect the Jewishness of Israel, they bar the owners of the lands on which the state was erected.

When Israel, aided by Britain and France, invaded Egypt in October 1956, the U.N. General Assembly in Resolution 997, approved November 2, 1956, called upon the invaders to withdraw their forces and reminded Israel that its invasion of Egypt was (in addition to being a violation of the U.N. Charter) a violation of the 1949 armistice agreement with Egypt.

The British and the French, as previously stated, bowed to the edict of the international communtiy and withdrew. But not Israel. So it became necessary for the U.N. and President Eisenhower to call upon her again and again. Only after securing the opening of the Strait of Tiran and the stationing of a U.N. force at Sharm al-Sheikh to keep it open did it agree to withdraw. And as the troops withdrew, they destroyed the highways behind them.

Israel's 1967 war against three Arab states was not only a violation of the 1949 armistice with the Arabs, as were many previous and subsequent raids into Arab territory, but was also a violation of Article 2 of the U.N. Charter, which says in the third and fourth paragraphs:

> All members shall settle their international disputes by peaceful means in such manner that international peace and security, and justice, are not endangered.
>
> All members shall refrain in their international relations from the threat or use of force against the territorial integrity or political independence of any state, or in any other manner inconsistent with the purposes of the United Nations.

As we have seen, Israel occupied large Arab territories in 1967. She is still in occupation of these territories, except for a small sliver on the eastern bank of the Suez Canal and a smaller one in Syria. This continued occupation not only violates Article 2 of the U.N. Charter and the 1949 armistice agreements but also defies Security Council Resolution 242, adopted back in 1967 and affirmed in October 1973. It will be recalled that Resolution 242 says that "the acquisition of territory by force of arms is inadmissible." But Israel has not withdrawn and insists on keeping at least several important areas in Egypt, in the West Bank of Jordan, and in Syria and has been establishing new Jewish settlements in various parts of these territories. And where Jewish settlements are established, Israelis say, the Israeli flag must remain.

Since the adoption of Resolution 242, the U.N. has adopted a score of resolutions, some condemning Israel for repeated attacks on Jordanian and Lebanese villages and her attack on the Beirut International Airport in which over a dozen Lebanese civilian airliners were destroyed; some directing her to permit the 1967 war refugees to return to their homes; some condemning her for violation of human rights in the occupied territories and for her violation of the Geneva Convention, which deals with the duties of an occupying government toward the civilian populations. But Israel has defiantly ignored all these resolutions. Tel Aviv has also turned a deaf ear to a General Assembly resolution adopted March 4, 1969, reaffirming the inalienable rights of the new Palestinian refugees to return to their homes. Tel Aviv has ignored also a Security Council resolution of July 3, 1969, that "censures in the strongest terms all measures taken to change the status of the city of Jerusalem."

As reports kept coming to the U.N. concerning violatons of human rights, the Assembly decided to send a committee to investigate the charges. Tel Aviv refused to allow this committee to enter Israel. Amnesty International tried to investigate charges of maltreatment of prisoners, but it, too, was denied admission to Israel.

It thus appears that the successive Israeli governments have faithfully adhered to Ben-Gurion's dictum; "Force of arms not formal resolutions will decide the issues."[26]

---

26. David Ben-Gurion. *Rebirth and Destiny of Israel.*

XXVII

The Triumph of the P.L.O. and Yasser Arafat

In the early days of the conflict, the United Nations was generally tolerant toward Israel and followed America's lead when the votes were cast. Since the 1967 war, however, the members have gradually become more and more disillusioned with the conduct of the "bastion of democracy in the Middle East" and its defiance of international law, the U.N., and the U.N. Charter. The admission into the U.N. of the newly independent Arab and African states and of the People's Republic of China—which had always been a strong backer of the Palestinians—encouraged the Assembly to assert its independence and to cease to meekly follow the American policy of "pampering Israel," as one delegate put it.

The Assembly at long last realized that peace in the Middle East depended not only on Israeli withdrawal from the territories occupied in 1967, a matter which has been and still is the subject of resolutions, mediations, etc., but also on the settlement of the basic question that caused all the Arab-Israeli wars. So it began, cautiously, to delve into the roots of the problem in the hope of finding a solution that could bring true and lasting peace.

At first timidly and with circumlocution but later boldly the

General Assembly, now made up of the representatives of over 140 nations, began to call for the recognition of the inalienable rights of the Palestinians and to demand their implementation.

In a resolution adopted on December 8, 1970, the Assembly said that it "recognizes that the people of Palestine are entitled to equal rights and self-determination in accordance with the Charter of the United Nations" and that the implementation of these "inalienable rights of the people of Palestine is an indispensable element in the establishment of a just and lasting peace in the Middle East." The Assembly thus correctly diagnosed the illness and even prescribed the medicine, but it did not provide it.

On December 6, 1971, however, the Assembly adopted a resolution that upheld the legality of the Palestinians' struggle for self-determination and said that it: "affirms man's basic human right to fight for the self-determination of his people under colonial and foreign domination."

The Assembly thus legitimized the armed struggle of the Palestinians and encouraged it. Finding itself helpless in dealing with defiant Israel, it in effect told the Palestinians that they must fight for their rights. and called upon all states dedicated to the ideals of freedom "to help them morally and materially."

On December 13, 1972, the General Assembly adopted a resolution that said, in part:

Affirms the right of the displaced inhabitants to return to their homes and camps;

Considers that the plight of the displaced inhabitants continues since they have not yet returned to their homes and camps;

Expresses its grave concern for the failure of the Israeli authorities to take steps for the return of the displaced inhabitants in accordance with the above mentioned resolutions;

Calls once more upon Israel immediately to take steps for the return of the displaced inhabitants.

As usual, Israel simply ignored this demand. So on December 7, 1973, the Assembly adopted a resolution that affirmed the above resolution and also said:

Declares that... the enjoyment by the Palestinian Arab refugees of their right to return to their homes and property, recognized by the General Assembly in resolution 194 (III) of 11 December 1948, which has been repeatedly reaffirmed by the General Assembly since that date, is indispensable for the achievement of a just settlement.

Of course, the Israelis had known this, and thousands of them had been demanding at least some compromise on the problem of the disposeessed Palestinians. But their government had been adament. So this resolution, too, fell on deaf ears in Tel Aviv.

The final communiqué of the June 1973 summit conference in Washington between the president of the United States and Secretary General Brezhnev declared that the settlement of the Middle East problem "should take into due account the legitimate interests of the Palestinian people." A similar statement was made in the communiqué issued at the end of the July 1974 Moscow summit meeting between the president and the secretary general. In a speech before the U.N. General Assembly on October 2, 1974, the deputy foreign minister of China said: "The restoration of Palestinian national rights and the recovery of the lost Arab territories form an integral struggle. There can be no settlement of the Middle East question so long as the lost Arab territories are not recovered and Palestinian national rights are not restored."

So the three superpowers, in their individual capacities, uphold the national rights of the Palestinians. India, the second most populous nation, has always backed the Palestinians and has not recognized Israel.

The high point in the history of the Palestine Liberation Organization came in 1974. An Arab summit held at Rabat in October of that year decided to recognize this organization as the official and sole representative of the Palestinians. This was done in the presence of King Hussein of Jordan, who, prior to the 1967 war, reigned over both banks of the Jordan River, and whose country—East Jordan or Transjordan—contains more Palestinian refugees than native people.

Naturally, His Majesty felt that he had been let down by his fellow Arabs. And knowing how Israel and Secretary Kissinger felt toward the P.L.O. and their guerilla activities, he thought that this decision was a mistake and said so. But, recalling that Washington's promises of protection and seven years of endeavor on his part, which included several visits to Washington, to regain control of the West Bank availed him nothing, he calmly took the decision in his stride.

Yasser Arafat and his followers expressed their jubilation and their gratitude to the assembled leaders of the Arab world.

On the heels of this victory, which already has started to wear off, the P.L.O. scored a much greater one.

The U.N. General Assembly during its 1974 session, which began in September and ended in December, included in its agenda the "Question of Palestine," previously discussed under such headings as "Refugees" or the "Situation in the Middle East," and adopted a number of resolutions, including the following:

Calls once more upon Israel immediately to: (a) Take steps for the return of the displaced inhabitants; (b) Desist from all measures that obstruct the return of the displaced inhabitants, including measures affecting the physical and demographic structure of the occupied territories.

Reaffirms the inalienable rights of the Palestinian people in Palestine, including (a) the right to self-determination without external interference; (b) the right to national independence and sovereignty.

Reaffirms also the right of the Palestinians to return to their homes and property from which they have been displaced and uprooted, and calls for their return.

Further recognizes the right of the Palestinian people to regain its rights by all means in accordance with the purposes and principles of the Charter of the United Nations.

Appeals to all states and international organizations to extend their support to the Palestinian people in its struggle to restore its rights in accordance with the Charter.

The Assembly thus not only sanctioned the P.L.O. guerilla war against Israel but also once more called upon the world to help it. It also said aloud:

Emphasizes that full respect for and the realization of these inalienable rights of the Palestinian people are indispensable for the solution of the question of Palestine.

Recognizes that the Palestinian people is a principal party in the establishment of a just and durable peace in the Middle East.

Having sanctioned the guerilla activities of the Palestinians, the Assembly then followed the Arab summit decision and recognized the P.L.O. as the representative of the Palestinians and invited its chairman, Yasser Arafat, to address it on the "Question of Palestine." This infuriated Israel and its supporters in the United States. The Jewish Defense League leaders vowed to kill Arafat to prevent him from appearing before the Assembly. A crowd, estimated at one hundred thousand Jews, assembled in front of the U.N. building in New York City to hear speeches by former Foreign Minister Eban and Defense Minister Dayan of Israel and U.S. senators Jackson and Javits and to shout anti-P.L.O. and anti-U.N. slogans in hope of causing the Assembly to alter its stand.

Despite the huge demonstration and the intensive lobbying by Israel, by American Zionists, and by the U.S. Government, the resolution to invite the P.L.O. spokesman was approved by a resounding vote of 105-4. The four dissenters were Israel, the United States, Bolivia, and the Dominican Republic.

Twenty nations abstained on the ground that to hear a speaker who does not represent a government was unprecedented. This was inaccurate. In May 1947, the General Assembly invited the Jewish agency and the Arab Higher Committee to speak on Palestine.

Once again the U.S. found itself practically alone allied with Israel.

Security for Arafat was very tight. Not only the Palestinians took the Jewish Defense League's threat very seriously but also the U.S. State Department and the New York City police did. To insure Arafat's safety, a helicopter lifted him from his plane to the roof of the U.N. building. After delivering his speech, he was taken back to his plane the same way.

To give Mr. Arafat and his supporters more cause for jubilation and to add to Israel's chagrin, the president of the Assembly, Algerian delegate Bouteflika, and the delegates present gave him the kind of reception usually reserved for heads of state. Then they followed that up by voting to allow a representative of the P.L.O. to attend all U.N. sessions as an observer (without a vote).

Arafat's speech was masterful but unrelenting. He said that he came "with an olive branch in one hand and a gun in the other," and then he pleaded with Israel not to let this olive branch drop from his hand. But the peace he offered was the same that the Zionists had rejected back in 1947 and still reject—a secular, democratic state in all of Palestine in which Jews, Moslems, and Christians would have equal rights and protection—which would mean an end to the Jewish state called Israel.

The Israelis, as might be expected, laughed at this "peace" offer. Moreover, they said that they would never negotiate settlement of the problem with Arafat or his P.L.O. They and their Jewish American supporters vehemently criticized the U.N. for its action. Complaints against "the tyranny of the majority" filled the air, and Zionist speakers and writers suggested withdrawal of America from the world's peace-keeping body. Majority rule became anathema to the Jews, who had often fought for it and still do, but they did not like it at the U.N. Back in 1947 when the Arabs opposed and the Zionists supported the U.N. partition resolution, Zionist propaganda adopted and stressed the slogan "Save the United Nations."

Returning to his base, Arafat and other guerilla leaders renewed their attacks against Israel which had been temporarily suspended. Israel, as usual, answered with air, tank, artillery, and even gunboat attacks against villages and Palestinian refugee camps in Lebanon.

This process of guerilla attacks followed by massive Israeli retaliation has been going on for some time now. The result has been the destruction of many Lebanese villages and the death of hundreds of Lebanese and Palestinian civilians.

The triumph of Arafat and the Palestinians at the 1974 session of the U.N. General Assembly was a great moral victory. But it achieved nothing. The "Question of Palestine" remains to be settled. But how and when?

XXVIII

Peace: Is It Possible?

It is sheer foolhardiness for anyone today to think that he can formulate a peace plan that both Arabs and Israelis will readily accept. In 1972 this writer, in the course of a lecture to an Arab audience in San Francisco, commended President Sadat of Egypt for continuing the cease-fire on the Suez Canal and expressing willingness to end the war with Israel. He was vehemently attacked by a couple hotheads. The critics were voicing the sentiments of the extremist Palestinian Resistance Organization, whose motto still is "Revolution until Victory."

Two weeks before this incident, high Israeli officials told him that it was "too early to talk peace." And there are people in Israel who prefer territory to peace. These people have been arguing that Israel should not withdraw from the occupied territories even though it means more war.

Most Israelis like to keep Old Jerusalem because they aspire to rebuild Solomon's Temple on its historic site. They forget that the Moslem Haram El Sherif, which contains the Dome of the Rock and the Mosque Al Aqsa,[27] highly revered by

---

27. In 1969 an Israeli set this mosque on fire, apparently hoping to hasten the rebuilding of the temple. But he only caused the whole Islamic world to rise in protest. Israeli authorities said he was an Australian Christian, known to have mental problems.

The Dome of the Rock in Old Jerusalem, as seen from the Mount of Olives.

Moslems the world over, has been there for a thousand years. They forget also that Jerusalem is the most sacred Christian city. Other Jews want to keep Jerusalem because it reminds them of Jewish temporal glory during the time of David and Solomon some three thousand years ago. These people have the grandiose dream of expanding Israel's boundaries to include the entire area between the Nile and the Euphrates rivers. Naturally this empire must have Jerusalem for its capital. It is the knowledge of the importance of the place Jerusalem occupies in the minds and hearts of Jews that led the author back in 1948 to predict that the Jews would sooner or later attempt to seize it. (See Palestine Dilemma, p. 218.)

This strong Jewish feeling is not confined to the Jews in Israel. It is present among Jews in the Diaspora—"Next year in Jerusalem" is serious business with most Jews.

Of course, the Arabs, too, have strong feelings about Israel and the occupied territories. While they usually speak kindly of Jews as individual human beings and are very tolerant toward Judaism, the very word *Israel* makes many of them see red. An alert and "patriotic" customs officer in moderate and westernized Beirut delayed passing a package containing copies of a pamphlet printed in the United States because a map of the Near East on its cover contained the word *Israel*.

"We don't recognize Isreal," he said, and in his opinion that fact required banning of the pamphlet, which he did not even read.

Nearly every Arab (including Christian Arabs) feels that the return of Old Jerusalem to Arab control is absolutely essential for peace. It is to be borne in mind that the Arabs don't call it *Jerusalem*. Its Arabic name is Al Quds—*the Holy*, i.e., The Holy City. Not only Christians but Moslems from all over the Arab and Islamic worlds come to Al Quds to pray in its holy sanctuaries. The late King Faisal said a short time before his death that his foremost wish was to visit Jerusalem and pray in Al Haram before he died. It is reported that when Secretary

Kissinger saw him on December 14, 1973, and asked him to lift the oil embargo, the following dialogue took place:

Faisal: "What progress on Jerusalem?"

Kissinger: "Well, er, none yet."

Faisal: "No oil."

The same wish was expressed by his successor, King Khalid, in an address to the sixth meeting of Islamic Foreign Ministers held at Jedda in July 1975. He called upon the delegates present to work for "the liberation of Jerusalem." This conference, which had backed the Arabs against Israel at its previous meetings, reaffirmed its support and appointed a special committee on Jerusalem. The task of this committee is the implementation of U.N. resolutions on Jerusalem. The conference also called for the expulsion of Israel from the U.N.

In discussing various peace proposals with King Hussein in Amman, the author brought up the question of Jerusalem. His Majesty dismissed the subject with *"Al Quds ma nufarret beha."* (Jerusalem, we would never let go of her.) And remember, Hussein is very moderate.

When the record of the song *Al Quds* sung by the famous Lebanese (Christian) girl Fairouz is played, tears roll down from the eyes of strong men.

The Arabs have always considered Jerusalem a holy city. Founded by the Canaanite Arabs about five thousand years ago, it was early made a center for the worship of the One God. Chapter 14 of Genesis says that when Abram (or Abraham) came to Palestine and struck camp in the vicinity of Jerusalem, the city was then—four thousand years ago—a center for the worship of God. Its king, Canaanite Melchizedek, was also "priest of God Most High."

The founder of Islam, Mohammed, at the beginning of his mission directed his followers to face toward Jerusalem at prayer. When the Khalifa Omar came in A.D. 637 to accept the surrender of Jerusalem from the patriarch Sophronius, he did not enter it with military pomp and fanfare. He entered it walking on foot as a humble and devout pilgrim, not as a conqueror. These facts, plus the facts that Jerusalem contains Islam's and the world's most beautiful religious structure, known as the Dome of the Rock and the Mosque Al-Aqsa, located in Al Haram Al Sherif, (*the Sacred Precinct*) give the city a unique place in Islam. Its sanctity is surpassed only by Mecca and Medina, the cities where the prophet lived and died.

Although emotionalism and chauvinism are rampant in both camps, there are, nevertheless, thousands there who have kept their heads, who are reasonable, fair, and, above all, realistic. These people have not been in the driver's seat, but their voices are becoming louder and louder. It is on these people that we ultimately must pin our hopes for peace, and we must actively encourage them. Of course, though they may be reasonable, these people are not altogether unbiased and fair. They are, like the majority of those around them, involved, and involved persons cannot be entirely unbiased. As Oscar Wilde put it, "It is only about things that do not interest one that one can give a really unbiased opinion, which is no doubt the reason why an unbiased opinion is always valueless."

But bias is a matter of degree. The people we are referring to are, of course, biased but they are not totally blind to the facts of life.

In speaking of a Middle East peace, a "political" settlement is meant that must include a measure of justice as large as it is possible to achieve under present conditions. It must be borne in mind that absolute justice is not always possible, not even in the courts of justice. The object is to reach an agreement that of necessity includes compromises in order to put an end to bloodshed and to establish security for all.

Having shown that Israel was illegally established by force, we now call upon the Arabs to forget its illegality and accept its existence as a fact of history. But we also call upon Israel to recognize the Palestinians' inalienable rights in Palestine—

173

rights that are recognized by the United Nations, the world organization for law and order, and by its individual members. Recognition of Israel by the Arabs and recognition of Arab rights by the Israelis are essential to an agreement that will put an end to the half-century-old struggle. Moreover, the following facts should be borne in mind:

1. Both leading superpowers—albeit for different reasons—and Western Europe back the continued existence of Israel. The chances for the Arabs to destroy her by force within the foreseeable future are, therefore, practically nil. As President Sadat of Egypt is quoted as having said during a visit to Quwait in May 1975, Israel is "a reality" that the Arabs must accept.

2. Israel cannot keep the territories occupied in 1967 and hope for peace. The very moderate Arab leader King Hussein, during one of his visits to Washington in quest of peace, said: "Israel can have these territories or peace. But cannot have both."

3. There can be no peace while half the Palestinians remain homeless refugees, most of them outside of Palestine. This fact is recognized by the world community.

4. Israel cannot impose peace on the Arabs by force of arms even if she wins another battle or two.

5. The Israelis should recognize that their state is not viable economically unless they make peace with the Arabs. We said this over a quarter century ago in *Palestine Dilemma*, and the past three decades have proved it. Despite Herculean efforts to remain solvent, Israel today is practically bankrupt. Despite what is said about her economic and industrial "progress," Israel has never had a single favorable trade balance. The cost of living has gone up 75 percent since the 1973 war. Despite heavy taxes and forced loans at home and the sale of Israeli bonds abroad and contributions from American Jews, the Israeli pound (originally worth $4.00) has been devalued several times since that war until today it is worth 14 cents. On per capita

174

basis, its public debt is the highest in the world.

6. Israel has survived so far only because of the generous economic, military, and political support of America. But history knows no nation that survived indefinitely on foreign aid. Already the demand for ending the folly of throwing away billions to convert friends into foes is growing louder.

7. Contributions (tax exempt) from American Jews, which have been very generous, are no longer enough. Israel's dependence on the U.S. Treasury was in the past expressed in millions. Now it is told in billions. The Jews in America are beginning to protest when the U.J.A. or the Israel Defense Fund collectors approach them. If the tax exemption granted these organizations is withdrawn, as it should be because their collections are for political and not for charitable purposes, we wonder how generous they would be.

The chances for peace improved considerably when Arab leaders came down from their high horses of the Khartoum summit manifesto of the "three nos"—"no negotiations, no recognition, and no peace"—with Israel and accepted Resolution 242, which requires termination of the state of belligerency and "acknowledgment of the sovereignty, territorial integrity and political independence of every state in the area," which, of course, includes Israel.

The Arabs have also publicly agreed to the "freedom of navigation" that the resolution requires and for which Israel alleged it started the 1967 war. Indeed, Egypt has already opened the Suez Canal to Israeli flagships.

Although this implicit recognition of Israel and ending the war against her is dependent upon Israel's withdrawal from the territories occupied in 1967 and "a just settlement of the refugee problem"—both of which conditions Israel has yet to accept—it is, nevertheless, a great change in Arab official policy and a great step toward peace.

It is believed that world opinion, Israel's almost complete

diplomatic isolation, the steady growth of Arab power, and the continuing slide downward of Israel's economy will eventually compel her to realize that it is in her interest to make settlement on the basis of this resolution.

Despite Israel's arguments concerning the meaning of the phrase "withdrawal of Israeli armed forces from territories occupied in the recent conflict," the debates in the Security Council indicate that this withdrawal must be complete, the absence of the article *the* or the word *all* in the English text notwithstanding. The French version of the resolution leaves little doubt about this. At any rate, this is the meaning placed upon it by the members of the U.N., including the United States and the Soviet Union. It is to be borne in mind that the resolution in question starts by "emphasizing the inadmissibility of the acquisition of territory by war." Israel's need of oil, for example, cannot justify her keeping the Egyptian Abu Rudeis oil field unless we revert to the law of the jungle. She has given them up pursuant to the second disengagement agreement with Egypt. (But Kissinger pledged her in addition to the annual $2.3 billion aid an extra $350 million a year as "compensation" and also guaranteed her delivery of oil in the event of an embargo.)

The requirement of "secure" boundaries in the first and second paragraphs which Israel has seized upon to justify continued occupation of some strategic parts of the territories in question applies to "every state in the area," and not to Israel alone. The Arabs, too, need "secure" or strategic boundaries. And the history of the struggle so far shows that they are in greater need of such boundaries than Israel is, since the latter has had superior military power. The Arab states have never invaded Israel.

And, after all, the only "secure" boundaries are those freely agreed upon by both sides. Those imposed by the victor in war only create *irredentas* and more wars.

As Secretary of State Rogers said, minor territorial adjustments that do not "reflect the weight of conquest" may be made, and indeed should be, but with the agreement of both sides.

The Arab summit held at Algiers in November 1973 authorized Egyptian President Sadat to negotiate a peace settlement with Israel but laid down two "paramount and unchangeable conditions": "Evacuation by Israel of the territories occupied by Israel in 1967, and first of all Jerusalem" and "reestablishment of full national rights for the Palestinians." Implementation of the first condition is easy to do without derogation of the sovereignty, independence, or Jewishness of Israel. It simply requires her to go back to the 1967 lines. Implementation of the second condition, however, is another matter. Liternal and complete reestablishment of the "national rights of the Palestinians," the first of which is repatriation of the refugees, means the elimination of Israel. Do the Arabs really expect to attain this now?

The P.L.O., the most representative Palestinian body, says it is fighting for repatriation of the refugees and the establishment in all Palestine of a democratic, secular state in which Jews, Moslems, and Christians shall live together in peace and equality. We wonder if this dream is possible after all the fighting that has taken place. Would not Palestine become another Lebanon? And the people of Lebanon are all Arabs. True, this is more moderate than earlier declarations by Arafat's predecessor. But it is the same old "one unitary government for all of Palestine" proposed by the Arabs back in 1947 and rejected by the Zionists when there was no Israel and the Jews in Palestine numbered only 650,000. Today, with the Jewish state firmly established and challenging the Arabs to battle and the power of the United States solidly behind her, is it realistic to expect the Israelis now to give up all their gains and say: "The partition of Palestine was a mistake. The expulsion of the Arabs was wrong and they all should come back so we both, Jews and Arabs, can live together in peace"?

The time will come when the Jews in Palestine will say

something like that. History usually corrects its mistakes. "Nothing is ever settled until it is settled right." But this often takes time. Israel will in time have a change of heart. But this change will come about mostly because of conditions within the state, or because of a change in America's policy, or both, and not because Arabs demand it. And remember that Israel thrives on war.

Besides Israel's desire to remain a Jewish state, there are great difficulties in implementing the program of repatriation. The face of the country has been greatly changed since 1948.

At a meeting in Jerusalem of a number of Arab and Jewish intellectuals, intended to promote social contacts and communication between the two peoples, one of the half dozen Arabs present stated that he was a 1948 refugee from the Jaffa area, that when the Arabs of the West Bank were permitted to enter Israel following the 1967 war, he went to see what had become of his home and orange grove, only to find both house and orange trees gone. In their place stood small apartment buildings.

How can we repatriate this man? Do we return the land that was registered in his name in 1948 to him and chase the Jews out? If we do this, will we not be creating another humanitarian problem—another crop of refugees? Or would not that start a new conflict?

The love of the Palestinians for their homes and for their land was repeatedly demonstrated during visits to their camps. During a visit to a camp in Jordan, I found myself with a camp officer, who was escorting me, in a hut about ten by sixteen that was occupied by an elderly woman, her daughter of about twenty, and three sons who were then out, perhaps with a commando outfit. The girl had invited us in for coffee as we were passing, and I eagerly accepted the invitation to get her views. I found both women as unshakable in their insistence on repatriation as the men I had talked to that day. They had been farmers in Palestine and wanted to go back to their "little place," as the old lady described it. They rejected an equivalent piece of land and a house in Syria or Iraq. "We want to go back to our own place," the young one kept repeating softly. "We don't wish to fight anyone, but we want to go back home."

A gun-toting boy I met on the dusty street said that he was from Saphphourya—ancient Sepphoris—and that the Israelis took his family's home and chased them out but that he was going to fight and get it back. (Sepphoris was completely razed in 1948, and its surviving inhabitants scattered.) He said also that he was a member of the Ashbal—Lion Cubs—and had completed training in commando tactics. He had been born in a camp in the Jordan valley, and in 1967 his family, along with others, were driven east across the Jordan river, thus becoming second-time refugees. He had never seen Saphphourya.

These people have an undeniable legal right to repatriation under international law, under U.N. resolutions, and under the Universal Declaration of Human Rights. But the problem is how to implement this right. Since the original 950,000 Arabs left their homes and lands in what is now Israel, almost three times that number of Jews have come and have settled in the homes and on the lands belonging to them. Do we expel these newcomers? Arab spokesmen now say that they do not want to do that. They say that they want to go back and live in peace with the Jews now there. But where?

Of course, many of them should and can be repatriated without trouble, but not all. Our Department of State has been talking in terms of one hundred thousand or possibly two hundred thousand only. But how about the rest of the one million six hundred thousand refugees?

Talk about a settlement of the question of Palestine these days centers around the creation of a Palestinian state in the West Bank and Gaza when these areas are evacuated by Israel. Assuming that such a state is created either as an independent sovereign state or as part of Jordan, how would that solve the problem of the Palestinians now in refugee camps? The answer is: hardly at all. There are over half a million refugees in these territories now. They have been there since 1948, and they have not been able to establish themselves economically.

Gaza is barely a hundred square miles of coastal land. It has some 250,000 refugees besides its original population. Gaza has not been able to absorb these refugees. The West Bank, too, is bulging with refugees who have not been absorbed in the area's economy. But the West Bank, with improvement of agriculture and the creation of small industries, could possibly absorb the refugees now there and perhaps a hundred thousand more. Gaza cannot do that. The people there now are in need of elbowroom. The improvement of the port of Gaza plus the provision of an adequate supply of water could possibly bring enough business there to provide employment for those now there and possibly a few more, but only a few.

We can assume that those Palestinians who have been integrated into the economies of Jordan, Syria, and Lebanon, and also those employed in the oil-producing states, will remain there permanently or for some years to come. But they are a fraction of the total.

We can also arbitrarily say that the 250,000 in Syria should be settled in that economically promising country. This was suggested by the author to a group in a camp near Damascus. The spokesman of this group said loudly, "If you give me the Azm Palace in Damascus, I will not accept it in place of my three-room house in Galilee." This attitude could possibly change if these people are given to understand that this is the best they can expect. So let us eliminate them from our consideration.

Having done all this, we will still have the refugees in Jordan and in Lebanon. And Lebanon for some time has been a big trouble spot—a big problem—for both Lebanon and Israel, a problem that must be dealt with without too much delay lest it cause a bigger explosion than all previous ones.[28]

For several years past, the author has bandied about an idea that at first was flatly rejected by the Arabs and ridiculed by the Israelis but that is becoming more and more acceptable in both camps—by the people but not by their officialdom. The idea is simple and easy to implement. It is not new. It is part of the U.N. partition resolution, which was pushed by the Zionists and by the United States but was swept under the rug on the heels of the 1948 Israeli victory. Because no one has yet proposed a better or more acceptable one, I shall offer it here.

Briefly the idea is: The so-called Gaza strip is part of one of the three sections of Palestine that under the partition resolution were to remain Arab and form the Arab state. Israel is required under Resolution 242 to evacuate it. (She would like to keep it to straighten out her southern border. But it has too many Arabs.) It is suggested that Israel evacuate also the southeastern part of the original section, which she occupied and annexed before 1967. This strip is desert country of little value to Israel. It was taken by Israel for military reasons. When peace comes, she would not need it. But it would give the Palestinians in Gaza a little more room to relieve the crowding. The area of this strip is only about two hundred square miles.

It is also proposed that Israel evacuate the northern section left to the Arab state by the Partition Resolution, which she took in 1948. This is western Galilee, which includes the cities of Nazareth and Acre and which is now home to most of the so-called Israeli Arabs, who have been a thorn in Israel's side, whether it is admitted or not. In December 1975, for example, the all-Arab city of Nazareth, despite government efforts to prevent it, elected as mayor Tewfik Ziad, an avowed com-

28. As we go to press, a very destructive civil war rages in Lebanon between the Christians and the Moslems. The Palestinians joined the Moslems.

181

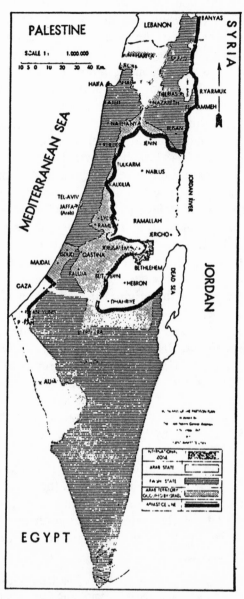

Proposed Arab state—white.

munist. Those Arabs had not become wedded to communist idealogy but were protesting against government discrimination, real or imagined, against their city. Giving up this section of territory, which is still largely Arab, would solve this problem. It would also make Israel more truly Jewish.

Israel shall keep the parts of the third Arab section (the West Bank) that she took in 1948. But the borders here should be rectified, taking into consideration the topography of the land and the welfare of the people—both Jews and Arabs— who live along the present armistice line. By "armistice line" is meant the 1949 armistice line, which the Arabs never recognized as permanent borders.

Jerusalem should be returned to its 1966 status: the western part to remain Jewish, the eastern to be returned to Arab control. This should satisfy both sides, since each will have a part of the coveted prize. Here it must be said that internationalization of Jerusalem is no longer feasible and neither side would like it.

As soon as possible, arrangements should be made to transfer the Palestinians now in refugee camps in Lebanon to Galilee, which should, of course, be made part of the proposed Palestinian state. Their transfer will stop their raids into Israel and would end the friction between them and the Lebanese people, which has erupted in shooting wars more than once.

Effort should be made to find homes and work in the proposed Arab state for the Palestinians now in the refugee camps in Jordan. Those who cannot be settled in this state or in Israel should be permanently settled in Jordan.

As we have seen, the United Nations and the heads of the Arab states have recognized the Palestine Liberation Organization as the sole representative of the Palestinian people. But Israel has refused to negotiate with this organization. She has even refused to attend a U.N. Security Council meeting on Palestine to which the P.L.O. had been invited. This situation, which threatens all peace negotiations, is reminiscent of the 1968 Paris peace conference on Vietnam. It will be recalled that the delegates to that ill-fated meeting spent weeks upon weeks debating the shape of the table and the position of the Vietcong representative's chair at that table. Of course, men who put so much store in trivia could not possibly agree on the substantive terms of peace. So the costly war went on for four more long years.

Israel says she objects to the P.L.O. being represented at a peace conference because this organization has not recognized her right to exist as a sovereign state. The United States, as usual, has backed Israel's stand even though Israel has not recognized the rights of the Palestinians in their own country.

What Israel really wants is to prevent the creation of an independent Palestinian state along her border which might prove to be troublesome. She prefers to turn the West Bank back to King Hussein, who is more likely to enforce security on her border.

Israel's concern for border security is understandable. Of course, the final settlement should provide for that, whatever the form of the Palestinian state. But is it Israel's prerogative to tell the Palestinians what form of government they shall have or who shall run that government?

True, the West Bank was part of the Kingdom of Jordan when Israel occupied it, and ordinarily it would be turned back to Jordan when peace comes. But King Hussein's war on the Palestinian guerillas in 1970 has made that rather difficult, although officially the Arabs of the West Bank are still Jordanian citizens and carry Jordanian passports. Indeed, until the Arab summit designated the P.L.O. as sole representative of the Palestinians, King Hussein had been helping the municipalities of the West Bank financially. And there are many there who are still loyal to him despite "black September."

To break the impasse thus created, let us forget about negotiations temporarily and proceed to create peace.

To hasten peace, to ascertain the wishes of the Palestinians concerning their future, to prevent any clash among the various Palestinian factions or between the Palestinians and King Hussein's government, and to assure the security of Israel's border until tempers cool off and the machinery of the new government is working smoothly, it is believed wise to place the territory evacuated by Israel under U.N. trusteeship for a period of five years or longer, if necessary. During this period the trustee shall administer the territory and shall also begin to transfer the refugees in Lebanon and Jordan to it and settle them and provide them with suitable employment.

When the time is deemed right, a plebiscite should be conducted to ascertain whether the people wish to be totally independent or whether they prefer to be united or federated with East Jordan.

This, of course, is to be a final settlement that contemplates recognition of Israeli sovereignty by the Arabs, who must also guarantee her borders against attacks by Palestinians.

Such settlement should be followed by ending the ruinous arms race and reducing the present armed forces on all sides to a sensible level, instead of seeking more lethal weapons in preparation for a more destructive war.

Of course, this pill is very bitter for either side to swallow. But the alternative is continued war, which could engulf us all. The aim of this book is to end that danger and bring peace to the land of the Prince of Peace.

ADDENDUM

Soon after becoming president in January 1977 Jimmy Carter tackled the question of peace in the Middle East, but soon found the going tough. The election of Menachem Begin to the premiership in May made the task even more difficult. Begin put a new interpretation on Security Council resolution 242, and claimed that the West Bank was "liberated" not occupied territory.

Secretary Vance, seeking Soviet support, met with Soviet Foreign Minister Gromyco. They drafted a peace plan to be presented at Geneva calling for Israeli withdrawal from Arab territories and recognition of the rights of the Palestinians. This aroused Israel's ire. American Jews sprang to her support. The White House was swamped with thousands of telegrams and 'phone calls. Foreign Minister Dayan met with Vance for seven hours. The administration caved in.

President Sadat, losing patience, in an impassioned plea in parliament for peace, said that he was ready to go anywhere for peace "even to Jerusalem". Newsman Walter Cronkite, sensing an opening, asked him if he meant this. Sadat replied that he did.

An invitation was promptly extended and Sadat went to the Holy City, prayed in Al Aqsa Mosque, and the next day, November 20, 1977, addressed the Knesset. He decried war and offered Israel not only peace but also recognition by the Arabs—the one thing which she had been seeking in vain for three decades. In return he asked for the return of Arab territories and recognition of Palestinian rights.

The world applauded and heaved a sigh of relief. At long last peace had come to the explosive Middle East. Even Begin saw "a foundation for peace" in Sadat's terms. But these terms were later rejected. Months of negotiations produced only an offer of partial withdrawal from Sinai, and limited autonomy for the Palestinians in the West Bank and Gaza under continued military occupation.

Sadat's bold move has been condemned by several Arab states and a number of Egyptian political and intellectual leaders. But at this writing, July 1978, he says he is still ready to consider a new offer by Israel, and President Carter is still trying, but under difficult conditions.